A publication of the

AMERICAN ASSOCIATION FOR HIGHER EDUCATION

A department of the National Education Association
1201 Sixteenth Street, Northwest
Washington, D.C.

G. KERRY SMITH, *Executive Secretary*

The American Association for Higher Education (AAHE), a self-governing department of the National Education Association, promotes higher education and provides a national voice for individual members. AAHE, founded in 1870, is the only national higher education organization open to faculty members and administrators alike— without regard to rank, discipline, or type or size of institution. It is dedicated to the professional development of college and university educators, to the achievement of their educational objectives, and to the improvement of conditions of service.

THE ARTS
in Higher
Education

THE ARTS
in

Foreword by HARRY RANSOM

Higher Education

Edited by

Lawrence E. Dennis &
Renate M. Jacob

Jossey-Bass Inc., Publishers
615 Montgomery Street • San Francisco • 1968

THE JOSSEY-BASS SERIES IN HIGHER EDUCATION

General Editors

JOSEPH AXELROD and MERVIN B. FREEDMAN
San Francisco State College

Foreword

Most of the answers to questions about commitment of colleges and universities to the arts are rooted in two plain facts. The first is that every university shares the responsibility. The second is that this commitment is inseparable from other university obligations. Even when institutional organization was unprepared to nurture it, the university has had the wisdom to celebrate creative imagination. This is because the arts are an essential element in the mind's attempt to make sense of human experience.

If this relationship has often seemed tangential, that condition has resulted from the accomplishments of artists outside the academic world—or in rebellion against it. These numerous historic exceptions, however, do not lessen the university's primary concern for the totality of culture.

Educational budgets face unavoidable priorities. As a result, too many American institutions—though they have seen our cultures steadily and seen them whole—decide to do something about them at some distant date when deficits become less pressing. Despite this budgetary procrastination, American campuses today are busily engaged with the fine arts. In the last thirty years, schools and colleges devoted to these disciplines have multiplied more than ten times, and degree programs—excluding the Bachelor of Arts—more than eighteen times. Equally significant are new educational opportunities for students who do not look forward to artistic careers. They are evident and they can be evaluated in the academic programs of university museums, conference centers, libraries, lectureships, and elective courses. To a whole population of students they have opened a world which only two generations ago was the special province of affluent students or determined undergraduate bohemians. Philanthropic and public support encouraging this development seems astronomical in its recent growth—until, of course, we compare that support with subsidies for the natural sciences.

The greatest encouragement to the arts on American campuses is perhaps to be found outside budgets and formal programs. The influence of writers and artists in residence has increased in ways that can never be reported as "semester hours" and "full-time equivalents." Friday-night painters, musicians, and writers have become a part of the life of the American college and university. Even transient voluntary associations, impromptu exhibitions, and fugitive publications have had their part in making academic history.

The arts need all the usual advantages of a university, including academic freedom. More than other disciplines, they need freedom from the academic. Without guarantees of that additional independence, they start with the safe, the agreeable, and the obvious; they end in banality and sterility. Up to now, the artist has avoided this threat by simply decamping. It will be worth the university's effort to persuade him to stay on his difficult, indefinite assignment and see it through.

The future of the campus arts will also depend in

part on the mobility of the artist, who needs to move about as much as the scientist or professional man. His movements will be less regular, of course, and much less easy to explain to the trustees. To accomplish anything like the necessary crisscrossing of experience, he will need most of all a flexible program of work in studio, on stage, and at the lecture desk. He must also be freed from the captivity of ancient proprietary customs which relegate great creation to convenient course bins and department cubicles.

Part of our problem will be the simple one of acknowledging great designs and complex relationships. Truly significant practices in the arts are not merely a matter of eye, ear, voice, or finger. Unless they are expressions of whole men and whole minds, they do not belong in the future university. If the arts must be paraded like Oscar Wilde's sunflower, or pampered like Madame Chuchinfleur's tomcat, universities must find some other means for participating in the study and creation of beauty.

For sensible progress in the future, the directions are clear. As the essays in this volume show, a sense of those directions will include profound respect for the tradition which joins the arts to education. It will also be committed to intelligent experimentation. In colleges and universities, or out of them, among multitudes or alone, the artist will fare according to his art. He cannot fare alone for great distances, for his art and the university make common cause.

It is for this reason that I welcome the appearance of this book, for it helps us explore the nature of that cause.

HARRY RANSOM
Chancellor
The University of Texas System

Austin, Texas
September 1968

xi

Preface

In June 1967, the American Association for Higher Education (AAHE), a department of the National Education Association, received a matching grant from the National Endowment for the Arts to conduct a study of access and barriers to the arts in higher education. This report to the Endowment completes the first phase of the project.

Lawrence E. Dennis, chancellor of the Rhode Island State System of Higher Education, served as director of the study, and Renate M. Jacob, of the Ford Foundation staff in Venezuela, was project assistant. As originally conceived, the project included the establishment under the aegis of AAHE of a National Advisory Commission on the Arts in Education, and the holding of a series of regional public hearings highlighting questions dealing with collegiate admissions practices as they affect access to the arts, the need for curricular reform in the arts at both the secondary and the higher education levels, and the value structure underlying public and professional attitudes toward the arts in schools, colleges, and universities.

However, due to limitations of staff time and delay in securing additional financial support required for the project, the project was revised to encompass the preparation of a series of background papers dealing with the arts in higher education; the holding of three seminars in Washington, D.C., on the subject, involving selected admissions officers and arts administrators; and the sponsorship of a special invitational conference on "Access and Barriers to the Arts in Higher Education," held in Chicago on March 4, 1968, in conjunction with the Twenty-third National Conference on Higher Education.

The American Association for Higher Education wishes to thank the Christian Faith and Higher Education Institute of East Lansing, Michigan, and the National Education Association for financial support that made it possible to match the first portion of the grant from the National Endowment for the Arts. Also, to the officers of the Endowment, and to the staffs of the National Art Education Association, the Music Educators National Conference, and the National Council on the Arts in Education, we extend our sincere appreciation for their continued interest in the project, which AAHE intends to carry forward. For valuable editorial suggestions, AAHE wishes to thank Joseph Axelrod and Mervin B. Freedman.

G. KERRY SMITH
Executive Secretary
American Association for
Higher Education

Washington, D.C.
September 1968

xiv

Contents

THE ARTS
in Higher
Education

I

Lawrence E. Dennis

The Arts Study Project

Are postsecondary educational opportunities as accessible to students interested in the arts—music, theater, art, and related fields—as they are to students seeking academic outlets in the natural sciences or social sciences?

Many observers of American life believe that a period of strong and significant artistic achievement in the United States may be at hand. To support this conclusion, they cite the enactment by the Eighty-Ninth Congress of the law establishing the National Foundation on the Arts and the Humanities, the rapidly growing number of state and municipal arts councils, and an increased public interest in museums, symphonies, community theaters, art institutes, and other cultural activities. When the National Council on the Arts was set up under White House auspices, Howard Taubman of the *New York Times* wrote that the arts in America are "rid-

1

ing the wave of the future," and said that he perceived the Council's primary function was "to educate the public in the meaning and value of the arts to the nation."

Such optimism may be premature, in the opinion of National Endowment for the Arts officials and American Association for Higher Education (AAHE) leaders who began discussing the new study project in 1966. For whether or not the "wave" becomes a reality will depend, of course, *not* primarily on government policies and programs, but rather on what is done by way of support for the arts in institutions of higher education. The chief educative responsibility for helping the nation bring its cultural potential to full flower and for developing more discerning audiences for the arts rests squarely on the shoulders of those who shape programs of resident instruction, research, and continuing education in junior colleges, colleges, and universities. If the creative arts are to flourish in this country in the decade ahead, the campuses must lead the way.

We already know largely what the American society of the 1970's will look like. It will be:

First, a learning society (witness the growth in collegiate, graduate, professional, and adult education programs);

Second, a technological society (witness the impact of automation and cybernetics on the national economy and on the configuration of industry and the service professions);

Third, an urban society (witness the growth of population in metropolitan areas and the changes in transportation patterns and living habits);

Fourth, a media-centered society (witness the continued social impact of television and the revolution in film-making);

2

Fifth, a leisure society (witness the trend toward shorter work days, a shorter work week, and extended vacations).

Given those premises about the future, it would be logical to expect that the arts would already be taking their place at the center of collegiate life, in both the curriculum and the extracurriculum, alongside of social studies, technology, and the sciences. But is this happening? Are enrollments in fine arts courses showing any significant increase relative to other areas? If so, what is being done to spur the trend? If there is no trend, what are the reasons?

If the campus climate for the arts is, indeed, negative—as this line of inquiry assumes—are admissions practices at fault? Do entrance requirements discriminate *against* students with special interests in art, music, theater, and related fields? The United States Commissioner of Education, among others, contends that such discrimination does, in fact, exist. In a commencement address at Ohio State University in June 1967, Harold Howe put the charge as follows:

> We should make the university environment congenial for the future artist, as well as for the active professional. This means revising the college admissions process. As now practiced, this screening rewards the academically talented high school student at the expense of the artistically talented. College admissions requirements and the achievement tests that help admissions directors make their decisions rarely reflect any interest in nonacademic, artistic pursuits. A high school student with a genius and obvious talent for painting rarely receives any credit for this talent from college admissions officers. The most you can say about his artistic ability is that it won't positively *hurt* him—as long as he got a "B" average in everything else, including driver-training and personal

hygiene. The notion that the aesthetic sense is crucial to the quality of a person's future life, and hence to his education, is not reflected in the standard admissions process today.

Can such allegations be effectively challenged? If not, what can be done to end such discrimination? And who should act to do so? Where are the critical pressure points for initiating needed changes in the admissions cycle?

To pursue the issue further: Does the college preparatory or academic-track pattern followed in high schools by those who want to go to college have a negative or depressing effect on creativity and interest in the arts? Should more formal credit be given for secondary school work in the arts? Are high school and college programs in the arts adversely affected by the fact that students who may want to enroll in them feel they do so at their peril— since those subject matters are thought to be outside the mainstream of formal education? Are college admissions tests weighted against creativity and the arts? Whose responsibility is it to effect changes in attitudes bearing on the arts at the secondary and college levels?

What can and should the federal government, the major foundations, institutions of higher learning, educational organizations, professional societies, and educational research agencies be doing to increase access and lower barriers to the arts in postsecondary education? Should the chief focal point of concern in higher education be (a) educating the general student in the arts—that is, broadening opportunities for educating an audience for the arts—or (b) educating the professional student in the arts—that is, preparing young men and women for careers in art, music, theater, and the like? Or should there

4

be—can there effectively be—focus on *both* these functions?

What do guidance counselors perceive education in the arts to be and how can the needs of education in the arts be made more evident to counselors? What do we know (or not know) about secondary institutions that give credit in the arts? How much attention do college admissions officers pay to the so-called "Carnegie Unit" system? What can state departments of education do to encourage greater participation by high school students in the arts; and how may certification procedures be altered to stimulate college education in the arts? Are there many good programs of general education in the arts in secondary schools? In junior colleges, colleges, and universities?

Since it took an international incident, namely, the appearance of Sputnik, to stimulate the development of science education, is education in the arts destined forever to have second or third priority behind science, technology, and social studies? What research is being done by the College Entrance Examination Board and the Educational Testing Service to determine whether college tests do indeed discriminate against people with talent in the arts? Does it take a good *professional* faculty in the arts to develop a high-quality program of *general education* in the arts? How can general education in the fine arts serve the goals of liberal education? How can closer liaison be effected between general and professional education in the arts? What can state councils on the arts do to facilitate educational development in the arts?

What precise enrollment figures do we have concerning growth of numbers of arts teachers and popularity of arts courses in colleges and universities? What do we know about the supply of teachers in the arts? What do we

5

know about the production of experimental and innovative instructional materials in the arts? Are there models of continuing education programs in the arts that might be relevant for undergraduate instruction programs? What do we know about programs of advanced placement in the arts, and are they worth encouraging? What actually do we know at this juncture about "creativity" and where is the best research on the subject being done? How do the arts relate to the "total quality of existence of American life?" What role can the National Endowment for the Arts play in encouraging development of both general education and professional education in the arts?

These questions are among the principal concerns of the AAHE Arts Study Project, initiated in mid-1967, after a preliminary seminar had been held in Washington, D.C., in late 1966 to discuss a background paper, "The Arts and Access to American Higher Education," prepared by Lewis B. Mayhew of Stanford University. In its first phase, the study spanned most of the 1967–68 academic year. The project director commissioned four background papers to deal with basic philosophical and educational problems relating to the arts in American education. (Mayhew's essay as well as the four commissioned papers are included among the chapters of this volume.)

In Washington, D.C., early in 1968, two further seminars provided the AAHE project staff with technical advice bearing on the status of the arts in higher education. Participants—leading admissions officers, registrars, deans of arts schools, and college presidents and vice-presidents—centered their attention on issues involved in college admissions practices affecting the arts.

A special invitational session of the National Conference on Higher Education, sponsored by AAHE in Chicago, March 3–6, 1968, devoted itself to discussing the

6

issues highlighted by the study. The special session heard summaries of the four commissioned papers, and discussion concerned activities that various organizations and agencies should undertake to increase post-secondary educational opportunities in the arts.

The purpose of these meetings was to explore the allegations that the fine arts are not now at the center of college life, and that there is overemphasis on science and technology in the curriculum at both secondary and higher education levels. Growing concern has been expressed by educators and artists that the arts are not playing a sufficiently vital part in American society, and that this is reflected in academic culture. Whether colleges are concerned with the obviously gifted and highly talented student who wants to embark on a professional career in the arts or with the much more complex problem of the general student who wants to be better informed and more appreciative of the arts, there has been increasing alarm at the negative and discouraging effect that admissions procedures exert on the arts.

Discussion at all three meetings—the seminars in Washington, D.C., and the special invitational conference in Chicago—focused on the following major areas: admission and testing, the general climate toward the arts in education, the need for curricular reform in the arts, and suggestions as to how schools, colleges, and universities might begin a concerted effort to promote access and lower barriers to the arts in education.

Are there factors in the general climate of opinion affecting educational development in this country that make for a stultifying effect on the arts in educational institutions? If there is such an attitude, is it reflected in admissions policies and how?

The most important question was what effect, if

7

any, current admissions practices have on the fine arts at the college level. In this connection, the main concerns are identifying and encouraging young people with artistic talent to obtain a higher education, providing access to the arts in general education for the student with an avocational interest, and determining the extracurricular climate for the arts.

It is assumed that many students are interested in the arts as part of their general education, but because arts courses are not considered a factor in collegiate admissions, and in view of the great competition for admission, arts courses are being displaced at the secondary level in favor of scientific and other subjects that help the student gain acceptance at the college of his choice. Fairly extensive analyses have shown that entrance examinations ignore the entire dimension of creativity and general culture appreciation. Is this lack of art education requirements in fact detrimental and unfair to the student who displays an interest in the fine arts and related areas?

Is it possible to effect some special relationships between schools and departments in the arts and collegiate admissions officers so that procedures could be developed favoring conditional admission for young people with a particular talent in the arts?

Several persons attested to the fact that numerous campuses have had conspicuously successful arts programs, and closer investigation has almost always revealed the existence of some unique arrangement or relationship whereby leaders of arts programs and senior administrators have by mutual consent allowed the admissions offices more flexibility and latitude in their policies toward arts-oriented students. In such informal arrangements, the dossier of an applicant who reveals any kind of predilection toward the arts is taken out of the routine screening proc-

8

LAWRENCE E. DENNIS

ess and brought to the attention of the arts department for an early evaluation of the student's capabilities and potential for college work, so that his special talents can be brought into a meaningful relationship with admissions requirements. An informal check of seven universities revealed that six of them had such special arrangements. Thus there is a much broader cutoff range than is generally assumed, although most schools commonly do not release such statistics for fear of tarnishing their academic reputations. The assumption is given further weight by the fact that Educational Testing Service has for years discouraged a rigid cutoff score as the basis of an admissions policy, and that it believes that a test score should not be the only criterion for determining admissions. Information from admissions officers reveals that secondary school course work in arts programs is transferable if the student requests it, and that they pay more attention to the individual student's goals and capabilities than a superficial study of the testing tools employed would indicate.

Are students who are particularly capable in the arts generally deficient academically in other areas? Should such students be encouraged to attend special schools and conservatories or are they on the decline, and, if so, why?

The alleged existence of such special arrangements brought up the question of whether the artistically inclined student is intellectually deficient compared with other students. There is research evidence showing that youngsters in the visual arts do not perform as well as other students in the computational and verbal skills that are highly rated on entrance tests. Such data indicate that poor academic performance of artistically talented youngsters is due to different motivations and interests and temperament rather than to lower intelligence levels.

9

An obvious solution to this problem might be the enrollment of such highly gifted students in professional schools. However, professional schools rarely grant degrees, and in view of current social and economic pressure for advanced degrees most students prefer to attend liberal arts colleges. While museum schools and conservatories are excellent in their own right and while their education can be fully as good as that of degree-granting schools, they seem to be on the decline.

The future art student should not need to depend on concessions from admissions officers; rather, all tests should include elements of art knowledge and competence on an equal basis with academic subjects. It is assumed that many students who are highly talented in the arts do not have an equal opportunity for a liberal education because of the undue emphasis on science, and that they would be successful college students if given the chance.

Do the university community and the academic setting provide a hospitable climate for the professional artist?

This would seem to speak for the need to reevaluate the structure of the present educational establishment and the value structure of society as a whole. Looking at college admissions from a historic point of view, it becomes clear that admissions practices reflect societal values.

In the present structure, a student's high school record constitutes important evidence of his readiness for college. The high school student is therefore faced with a choice: his interest and talent may lie in the arts, but if he concentrates on this field his high school record will not be as good as it might be if he developed his studies around admissions requirements. The present structure is clearly not satisfactory, because a very important segment of our culture is neglected.

10

In connection with the high school record, the possibility of pressuring colleges into accepting Carnegie Units in the arts as an admissions requirement has been raised. In view of what the Carnegie Unit stands for and because there has been some question as to its validity and usefulness, there is some doubt as to its merits as a means of measuring competence and ability in the arts and other creative fields.

To clarify the discussion about "Carnegie Units," the following excerpts are quoted from a study conducted by the National Association of Secondary School Principals in its January 1964 *Bulletin:*

> The Carnegie Unit is a measure representing a year's study in any major subject in a secondary school. . . . It assumes that a satisfactory year's work in any major subject cannot be accomplished in less than 120 sixty-minute hours or their equivalent.
>
> Data presented in *Improving Transition from School to College,* a survey of college admissions practices, indicate that the majority of high schools and colleges still subscribe to the provisions of the Carnegie Unit as defined in 1909 by the Carnegie Foundation for the Advancement of Teaching.
>
> Further they indicate that approximately 60 per cent of colleges and 63 per cent of high schools still use the Unit method of evaluating pupil's work in high school. On the whole, there is more opposition toward the use of Carnegie Units on the part of high schools than there is on the part of colleges.

To the question as to why so many high schools and colleges still use the Carnegie Unit system, the answer is as follows:

11

A satisfactory substitute has not been clearly defined and agreed on. Another is that the Carnegie Unit has been administratively convenient and therefore easy to operate. Many teachers and administrators believe that certain kinds of objective measures of achievement will eventually replace the concept of serving time in the classroom which is an essential feature of the Carnegie Unit.

But there are three disadvantages to the use of the Carnegie Unit:

It [the Carnegie Unit] lends prestige to those subjects acceptable to colleges in terms of entrance Units, and discriminates against other subjects excellent in their own right but as yet unacceptable for Unit measure.

It tends to make inflexible the daily and weekly time schedules of the school, for the Carnegie Unit nourishes the idea that a class should meet one period a day five times a week.

It restricts the development of a more functional curriculum based upon students' abilities, interests, and life-needs, because it has been difficult for the high schools to obtain units of credit acceptable to the colleges in certain more functional subjects.

What is the current status of tests? Does the Carnegie Unit actually impose a handicap in evaluating a student's potential in the arts? How much attention do college admissions officers pay to the Carnegie Unit?

Although college tests do not actually discriminate against the arts, they do not encourage identification of the student with potential in the arts. Tests are designed to identify those who have prepared themselves to fit into

12

the model of higher education that now is not arts-oriented.

There is general agreement that professional testing services have an obligation to devise artistic aptitude and achievement tests, but this is easier said than done. Test designers need to know what dimensions of mind and behavior are to be assessed, and the practitioners in the field themselves cannot agree about these dimensions. The main problem lies in the difficulty of predicting and grading the performing arts, because human talent is so extremely complex and diverse. Furthermore, humanists resist the idea of imposing quantitative measures on artistic and creative qualities, even if they *can* be isolated. Much useful work is, however, now under way in the effort to define the dimensions of creativity.[1]

Are enrollments in arts courses in colleges and universities growing?

There is an increase taking place in theater, symphony, and museum attendance across the country. Is this growing interest in the arts and related areas also reflected in increased enrollments in arts programs in colleges and universities? A study reported in *School and Society* (January, 1968) indicated that in thirteen schools there has been an increase of 41 per cent in enrollments in schools of music, fine arts, and applied arts. In recent years, increases of 7.4 per cent, 5.1 per cent, and 6 per cent have been reported.

Do economic factors in our society continue to lessen motivation for entering the arts?

There is no doubt that economic factors adversely affect the number of students entering arts fields. When the day comes when a percussionist out of school two years can join the Chicago Symphony—or any symphony—at

13

$12,000 a year, or when a student still in school is approached by a ballet company to play first oboe at $300 a week, economics will no longer be a deterrent.

Is the educational establishment governed by men and women with no particular commitment to the arts?

American society tends to value academic areas more highly than the arts. Clearly the universities do not accept the arts as central to the education of society. High school planning, curriculum development, and selection and training of teachers are so heavily oriented to the demands of colleges and universities that there is no reason to hope that their focus will change until the colleges themselves accept the arts as subjects of equal importance along with other academic fields. Some of the reasons for this general attitude are traditional. The minutes of a Harvard faculty meeting a hundred years ago reveal great resistance to the introduction of a science program. Today the arts, particularly the performing and practicing arts, are viewed with suspicion; they are not respectable academic fields. (Art history and musicology, on the other hand, are quite respectable.) A creative and talented teacher in the arts may not be acceptable as a member of the faculty because he lacks publications and other credentials. He cannot be measured the way a political scientist or economist can be.

How can one obtain a commitment to the goal of strengthening education in the arts from the educational leadership community?

In order for a national demand for general education in the arts to be created, many more people from all segments of society must be involved. The universities are now beginning, poorly perhaps, but with an increasing sense of commitment, to create an educational environ-

14

ment conducive to the pursuit of the arts as a serious subject. The presidents of major institutions should take a stand on behalf of arts programs of substance and quality in their schools and put pressure on admissions policies that would ultimately change the character of arts programs in education.

Are there models of outstanding programs in general art education?

Several models of higher education institutions that successfully incorporate arts programs, giving them equal status with other academic disciplines, were discussed. One such example is the new State University of New York, College at Purchase. This institution is attempting to synthesize the best features of the conservatory and the university. This synthesis will probably require eliminating the fifty-minute hour and restructuring the learning day now generally accepted in the traditional university schedule. The College will have broad liberal arts offerings and a professional arts center to which young people will be admitted on the basis of talent, regardless of their ability to meet normal admissions standards. However, all students not only must meet the requirements for a professional certificate but will take a considerable liberal arts program in addition to their professional work. It is hoped that most of them can be motivated to pursue a Bachelor of Fine Arts degree.

Hampshire College in Massachusetts is another model institution. Still in the planning stage, Hampshire is attempting to use the arts to serve the goals of a liberal education. Film will help increase participation by helping students understand what is being taught in the rest of the school. Hampshire College is committed to breaking down the barriers between the disciplines, not only within the humanistic fields, but between the humanities and sci-

15

ences as well. For example, ethnomusicology is a study that involves both the arts and the behavioral sciences.

What is the role of the guidance counselor in encouraging students to enroll in arts programs?

The guidance counselor's job should be to know what it takes to succeed in a given profession and to relate an individual's competencies to his college education. Instead, his job often seems to be interpreting college catalogs and, after checking a student's score on a given battery of tests, advising him whether or not he is likely to get into college.

Why is it important to have some educational exposure to the arts?

The function of arts programs, in the minds of most administrators, is to produce works of art; but this is the wrong reason. The reason these programs are necessary is that they are capable of making a unique contribution to a student's growth as an individual. A person is not whole if he cannot hear and cannot see and cannot interpret the experiences of hearing and seeing. Music, dance, the theater, painting, and the other fine arts—all hold some of "the joys of living" which are ends in themselves.

While discussing the dimensions of the AAHE study Project with various leaders in the academic community, it became increasingly clear to the Project staff that there are four general emerging areas of concern for the arts in higher education:

All institutions (junior colleges, four-year institutions, universities) need to be involved in developing general education programs in the arts for all post-secondary students. The general thesis here is that, as our society becomes more and more a "learning society" and a "leisure society," the post-secondary institutions need to assume active responsibility for developing public understanding and appreciation for the arts either in resident instruction or in other education programs.

Universities are now generally accepted, both by the public and by the artistic community, as logically the major training centers for professional artists. So assertively has the university assumed its responsibilities for the training of professional artists in recent years that it is now not possible to consider any other agencies in our society as having the resources and commitments necessary to serve as training centers for professional artists. Even the narrowly conceived, highly specialized, nonacademic professional schools are turning more and more to some kind of university affiliation. It is safe to predict that in the seventies, universities, in addition to the many academic and public service functions they already perform, will become cultural magnets attracting a wide range of professional artists to training and professional development programs under university auspices.

Four-year colleges and universities are fast becoming the major determinants of the preparation of teachers of art, music, and theater in secondary schools (and, in some instances, the junior colleges). To put it another way, the states—through their departments of public instruction—are rapidly disappearing as the licensing agents in the arts, and professional accrediting bodies associated with post-secondary institutions are taking over that function.

Over a long span, universities will probably emerge in our society as the major curators of the arts. Although the "museum movement" is growing rapidly in the United States, thanks in no small measure to stimulation from federal funds, some museums are already developing loose relationships with universities in order that each may take advantage of the other's resources. In the next decade or more, urban universities may logically bring museums under their wing and sponsor or cosponsor programs of education in the arts with those museums. This "curator" function of the university is not unrelated to its other public service functions, and does relate to both instruction and the pursuit of knowledge. The "university city" of the future will not be complete without the museums and exhibits needed to augment the educational programs; in fact, the great world's fairs in the last twenty-five years of this century will probably be held with the collaboration of the great international universities.

The American Association for Higher Education is publishing this report as a means of stimulating discussion of the many questions dealing with the arts in higher education that are reflected in the chapters that follow. Should the officers of the National Endowment for the Arts decide to continue to work with the American Association for Higher Education and other appropriate organizations in exploring ways by which barriers to the arts in higher education can be lowered and educational opportunities in the arts broadened, the initial AAHE inquiry will have served a most useful purpose.

If one or more of the educational foundations see fit to underwrite the establishment of a National Advisory Commission on the Arts (see Recommendation One in Chapter Seven), the American Association for Higher Education would be honored to join with similar organizations in sponsoring such a Commission and assisting it in its endeavors. Buttressed by the findings of the proposed Commission, the National Endowment for the Arts should be able more effectively to use its resources in developing long-term programs designed to broaden access to the arts at all levels of education.

Franklin D. Murphy has said, "It is quite clear that the people of the United States have directly or indirectly turned to their universities for a major commitment in the fields of social, cultural, and economic development. . . . I see in the precedents and in university history no reason why, if the will is there, the fine arts cannot be brought in as full and respectable parts of the expanding, changing American university. . . . If the university is unable to make the adjustments necessary in order to do this, it will be a sad day for the fine arts in the United States." It will indeed. The AAHE study is a modest attempt to alert the academic community to its responsibilities to make certain that "sad day" never comes.

Reference

1. See Paul Heist (Ed.), *The Creative College Student: An Unmet Challenge,* San Francisco: Jossey-Bass, Inc., 1968, where attempts to define and measure creativity are described in some detail.

II

Earl E. Edgar

Philosophy, Democracy, and the Arts

To claim an interrelationship of the values of democracy and the fine arts calls for an examination of the nature of those values and the extent to which they support one another. The nature of the contribution that the fine arts can make to a democratic social order, and democracy as an environment for the fine arts, are here explored. Conclusions drawn from such an inquiry should have important implications for education, for it is upon the basic values of a society that its system of education is founded, to the extent that the educational community understands and can realize those values.

The inquiry involves a more general problem, that of the functions of art. Vivas and Krieger have distinguished three general attitudes among those who have concerned themselves with the relationship of art and its audience.[1] There are those who regard art solely as an end in itself, its justification lying in the pleasure it gives the spectator. Others have considered art a means to either private or public improvement, or both, in religion, politics, morality, or truth. A third group has held that art can be a unique means to private or public improvement only if it is first conceived as an end in itself.

The chief merit of the first attitude is its emphasis on the fact that the aesthetic experience is one of life's final goods, that it is an ingredient in the good life to which social arrangements, including political organization, are or should be instrumental. This is said in order to clear the way for the position that the arts may be regarded also as a means to "public improvement," basically because the arts exist as part of the larger experience of individuals and societies and it is difficult to see how the reciprocal effects of art and society can be denied.[2] In what sense the values of the fine arts support democracy and how their influence is exercised, and what kind of environment democracy provides for the arts, remain, however, open questions.

Our problem is the relation of the fine arts to democracy conceived as the political expression of certain basic values. The values of democracy have been celebrated so often and for so long that it is difficult to get behind the clichés to the genuine meaning of the term. There are those, for example, who have found the central meaning of democracy in the concept of individualism,[3] but individualism, in fact, has at times taken the form of unbridled egotism, selfish pursuit of private advantage, and indifference to the welfare of others. In the history of democratic theory, however, individualism has referred to a complex ideal. It includes the concept of measuring the

21

worth of all social arrangements and institutions by the opportunities they afford the individual to realize his fullest potentialities. Paradoxically, perhaps, it includes both a sense of a common human fate and destiny, for it calls for respect for each individual, not on the basis of birth, breeding, or wealth, but just because of his humanity, and also an insistence upon the uniqueness of each individual, for it opposes the treatment of any person on the basis of traits ascribed to him as a member of some class or category. In the spirit of the Kantian injunction to treat each person always as an end rather than as a means, individualism implies that the individual's purposes should be his own; rather than being externally imposed, they should be purposes that are meaningful to him and to which he has given his voluntary commitment. From this viewpoint, the fundamental aim of education in a democratic society is to develop each individual to the point where he can choose and be responsible for his own goals and action. The process of rational persuasion, accordingly, becomes central to both the educational and political process; and the system as a whole involves respect for and protection of minority opinion and the guarantees of freedom of association, educational opportunity for all, and an independent press.

Implicit in the foregoing discussion of individualism have been the two values most frequently associated with democracy—freedom and equality. In the political sense, liberty has been conceived to be freedom to act under laws in the formulation of which the individual has had the right to participate and which are applied equally to all. Basic as this sense of liberty may be, it is hardly coextensive with the whole of life in which the issues of freedom are posed to the individual. In this wider sense, freedom, rather than being opposed, is achieved only through action within and for them. The issues of freedom provide the individual with the opportunity and the means through which his potentialities can be actualized—one of the genuine meanings of freedom. The more the individual is isolated from his society and culture, and the more meager the cultural and social resources that are available to him, the less freedom he can enjoy.

The idea of equality has already been suggested in the reference to a sense of a common human fate and destiny, and to the equal application of the laws. In the latter case its close association with the idea of justice becomes evident. Equality, in democratic theory, has been intended to mean an ideal, a set of rights, not an empirical generalization about human nature. Equality is basically a moral assertion, and the attempt either to prove or refute the equality of man as a psychological, physical, economic, or social fact has been one of the more futile exercises in political theory. Equality means equal rights (to "life, liberty, and the pursuit of happiness," in the classic phrase), equal access to and treatment by the courts, equal opportunity to develop one's abilities—all these buttressed by an equal voice in government, without which other rights could be eroded and liberty becomes a hollow piece of rhetoric.

A social order dedicated to such values is perhaps the most sophisticated and demanding type of social organization in existence; in brief evidence of which is the constant gap between the ideals of such a political organization and the actuality in societies generally recognized to be democratic. Attempts in recent years to establish democratic governments in underdeveloped countries have failed essentially because the conditions for the success of democracy were almost totally absent. The lesson of the very serious problems our own society is facing today

23

THE ARTS IN HIGHER EDUCATION

would seem to be that the difference between a democratic
society that is mature and experienced and societies that
cannot provide the conditions prerequisite for democracy
is a matter of degree, not of kind.

One of the conditions upon which democracy depends has been described by Francis Coker as the existence
of a "civic" sense among the people generally, which is
comprised of "a rational likemindedness and an imaginative sympathy that in some degree transcend economic
and cultural differences," along with a general disposition
to elect to high governmental office the kind of people
who act largely under the influence of such attitudes.[4]
This reminds us that constitutions are but words on paper;
if they are to "work," their provisions must be incorporated in the value system and behavior of citizens. The
requirements that democracy lays upon its citizens—obser-
vation of due process, submission to majority rule, concern for the common good, respect for the rights of others,
the use of liberty with responsibility, toleration of other
points of view and other ways of life—are requirements its
critics have asserted cannot be fulfilled in a society based
on popular sovereignty. Thus Plato declared democracy
to be the next to the worst form of government, tyranny,
and that it was bound, by its excesses, to lead to that political fate. Carl Becker writes of the "hard conditions" on
which those "gambling on democracy" can "win their
bet." Indeed, the democratic requirements demand a kind
of self-restraint on the part of citizens, the achievement of
which (insofar as it is achieved) becomes the more remark-
able as one reflects on the potentialities for antisocial,
aggressive, and neurotic behavior in human nature, ex-
acerbated today by life under conditions of modern industrial society and the tensions of international relations.

In short, democracy as an ideal demands highly

24

civilized behavior of its citizens. To the extent this is absent, substitutes must be provided, for example, laws that habituate people to the kind of restraints needed, and the threat of force that is implicit in the power of the state. However, we are only too aware today that in a viable society force must be the exception rather than the rule, and must be exercised in the context of social justice.

But that society is on safest ground which can depend mainly upon self-imposed restraints. For a democratic society this means the self-restraints arising out of a basic commitment to humane values: a respect for the rights of others and for human dignity—the "imaginative sympathy," in Coker's phrase, that transcends economic and cultural differences.

One of the basic sources for the development of such feelings and attitudes is experience of the fine arts as embodiments of man's longing for beauty, order, harmony, and creativity. Ordinarily our own experience of the depths and heights of human nature is limited and narrow. As a means of recreating in each new generation an appreciation of the humane values on which democracy rests, it would seem natural and inevitable to turn to the poetry, novels, and drama that, because they have explored all dimensions of the human condition, can deepen our understanding of mankind and his complex and varied potentialities; and to the painting, sculpture, and music through which the deepest human emotions have been expressed and released. These works of art themselves, as Gottschalk points out, are usually products of intense devotion, great fertility, and immense skill, monuments to human enormous strength and resourcefulness, and as such can remind us of "the heights of creative freedom and initiative of which man is capable and of the great potential for extraordinary accomplishments of the human being." We act, he points out, on the basis of what we sense and imagine, feel and think, value and cherish. If the fine arts can refine these bases of behavior, "making our capacities more able and our values more wide and discriminate, they constitute a discipline in decency and a modification of character from which decent social action can spring." [5]

Dewey makes the same point when he remarks that savage and civilized man are what they are, not by native constitution, but by the culture in which they participate. Acknowledging the effect of specific works of art upon a particular person or group, Dewey emphasizes rather the "massive adjustment of experience" that results from the total environment that the collective art of a time creates. In comparison with the influence of architecture, the novel, and drama on life, the sum total of the effects of all reflective treatises on morals is insignificant; compared with the influence of the arts, "things directly taught by word and precept are pale and ineffectual." [6] "Forms of poetry are forms of human life," Santayana writes. "Languages express national character and enshrine particular ways of seeing and valuing events. To make substitutions and extensions in expression is to give the soul, in her inmost substance, a somewhat new constitution." [7]

We are not talking about a "democratic" art, if such could be art at all. We are referring rather to an art that is honest to its own vision of human life; and we are saying that such art will perform a unique service to a democratic society. *It is our contention, in brief, that the fine arts and democracy are linked by an essential humanism that is shared by both.* Democracy in its various forms is the political expression of that humanism, and the arts have contributed to the development of the humanistic tradition and are one of the important means by which it may be maintained as a vital force. In a recent review of

26

the writings of the French authors Céline and Rebatet,[8] George Steiner claims to have found in these novelists examples of the coexistence of barbarism and the capabilities and sensitivities that make it possible to create great art. Steiner suggests that Sartre was wrong when he wrote that "no one could suppose for an instant that it would be possible to write a good novel in praise of anti-Semitism." That "a human being can play Bach in the evening, and play him well, or read Pushkin, and read him with insight, and proceed in the morning to do his job in Auschwitz and the police cellars," Steiner asserts, is "a fact, although one with which neither our theories of education nor our humanistic, liberal ideals have even begun to come to grips." We can only comment that we should imagine a world without the civilizing influence of the arts to be even worse than it now is. It seems obvious that fascism and Nazism came into existence despite, not because of, the artistic traditions in Italy and Germany, and that artistic freedom was, wisely from the point of view of the ruling powers, one of the casualties of these regimes, as it has been under the Soviets—a truth to which various Soviet novelists, poets, and composers could bear witness. Despite exposure to the arts, a person may, indeed, remain a barbarian: lack of receptivity, because of personal history or the presence of strong countervailing forces and consequent failure of educative efforts, is familiar. "It is still a superstition to believe that by some single piece of magic everything can be turned to gold," Gottschalk remarks. "And the arts certainly cannot do that."

From this point of view, more detailed remarks about the means by which the influence of the arts is exerted would be appropriate. The dangers of didacticism in the arts are well known, although they are more likely to be associated in our minds with examples of novels, dramas, and painting of questionable aesthetic quality than with Byzantine mosaics and the poetry of Lucretius and Dante. Perhaps Dewey is right, that what we resent in didacticism in the arts is not that it teaches, but its failure to teach; that our revulsion at any suggestion of teaching and learning in connection with the arts reflects rather upon an education that employs such literal methods that the imagination is excluded and the desires and emotions are not touched.[9] In any event, it is of the very essence of the manner in which art exercises its most significant influence on behalf of humane values that it be done, as Dewey puts it, "not directly, but by disclosure, through imaginative vision addressed to imaginative experience"; that it teach "as friends and life teach, by being, and not by express intent." Dewey emphasizes, moreover, that this Shelleyan emphasis upon the imagination is not merely the commonplace that a person's ideas and treatment of his fellows depend upon his power to imagine himself in his place. "The ideal factors in every moral outlook and human loyalty are imaginative," Dewey observes; this accounts for the historic alliance of religion and art, and is why "art is more moral than moralities," for "the moral prophets have always been poets even though they spoke in free verse or by parable." [10]

Phenix has drawn our attention to the support given to individualism by certain essential traits of the aesthetic experience itself: by the independence and concreteness of the art object, the intrinsic character of aesthetic values, and the creativity represented by both the artist and the appreciator of art.[11] The fruit of aesthetic experience is appreciation for the unique and unrepeatable, for the specific and individual, and we should foster the development of such appreciation if we are to counterbalance the impersonal outlook fostered by exclusive attention to abstraction, to similarities and conformities, that is the trademark of the scientific approach to the world. Phenix suggests that the dominance of abstractive science and technology and the preeminence of conceptual modes of thought may bear some responsibility for the prevalent depersonalization and collectivization of the modern world. Regarding the arts as a powerful support for individualism and defense against submersion in the mass, he suggests that one cure for the ills of modern society is the revival of interest in the aesthetic.

The art object is enjoyed, furthermore, not because it serves some purpose beyond itself, but in and of itself. If the color and form of a field of grain are taken as cues to practical activities—that a better kind of seed should be chosen, or that the time of harvesting is near—the perception is not aesthetic; the experience is aesthetic only if the colors and forms are enjoyed in and for themselves. As such, the aesthetic experience is essentially contemplative, its satisfaction consisting in the sheer beholding of the object. In the observer's respect for the "sovereignty" of the thing he beholds, Phenix finds a significant counter to modern man's obsession with control and his desire to subject everything to his will. The arts teach that "subjection and control do not have the only or the last word, that man needs also to come in humility to be taught, to become sensitive, to watch, listen, and savor, to gain awareness of manifold excellences and perfections beyond his own narrow and willful orderings of things." From the arts we can learn that it is important to let particular things be themselves, to value them for themselves and not for their usefulness to other ends. The arts remind us of "the richness and variety of the possible forms of things," Phenix writes, and serve as a protest against "every attempt to bring all existence under an arbitrary dominating will-to-power."

29

Serenity, a sense of present satisfaction, an experience of consummation are needs of human beings, and in serving such needs art supports freedom against tyranny.

Finally, Phenix remarks on the respect for creativity that is embodied not only in the artist's activity, but also in that of the appreciator whose participation in the values of the art object also requires a creative, not merely a passive, effort. This creativity of the arts, the making and enjoyment of beauty, contrasts with mechanization and routinization, with repetitive, purely habitual types of activity. Novelty, inventiveness, experimentation, and imaginativeness are the hallmarks of artistic creativity.

Running through Phenix's analysis is a contrast between the fine arts and the sciences that tends to become invidious. The two are certainly different modes of cognition, but are not necessarily antithetical. Although the arts have been uniquely associated with creativity, that is also a prized quality in any science that is seeking to transcend its historic triumphs. If Bertrand Russell is to be believed, a mathematical demonstration may have its aesthetic traits and satisfactions. Through the conceptualism of the sciences we can make and have made important human values more secure. Science and art, in the social sense, are or should be complementary, as society needs the knowledge provided by the scientist, but used in the service of values illuminated by the sensitivity and discrimination of the artist.[12]

Clearly a democratic society, particularly in a time of rapid change, must stress the value of creativity and its exercise by as many members of the society as possible. The traits that foster creativity include nondefensiveness, independence in value judgments, sensitivity to problems, capacity to tolerate ambiguity, and a display of strong aesthetic interests.[13] Creative capacities and psychological health are also very closely related.[14] An environment that fosters creativity is one that is nonauthoritarian and open, which describes a truly democratic social order; in turn, as creativity and psychological health are linked, creativity would appear to support the requirements of democracy. This is why it was somewhat dismaying, even if not altogether surprising, to learn from the work of Getzels and Jackson and of Torrance and his Minnesota associates that our schools have ignored, even punished, the creative behavior of children. Elementary school teachers have been found to exercise sanctions against creative children, and to rate them as less desirable pupils than children with high I.Q.'s. High achievers who have high I.Q.'s have been favored in schools, but not high achievers who are highly creative.[15] Here we have another example of the lag between the democratic ideal and its translation into educational terms.

The potentials of democracy as an environment favorable to the fine arts consist in its emphasis on shared values, its character as an "open" society, and the commitment to self-realization that is fundamental to democratic doctrine.

The emphasis on shared values is a feature of democracy made prominent in Dewey's educational philosophy.[16] Seeking to find, in existing groups, desirable traits in community life that could be bases for comparison and improvement, Dewey found these in some interest the group holds in common, and a certain amount of interaction and cooperative intercourse. From these Dewey derived his standards for the meaning of community. We must, he said, ask how numerous and varied are the interests that are consciously shared, and how full and free is the interplay with other forms of association. In a despotically governed state, he remarked, there is a com-

31

mon interest between governed and governors, but the activities the governors appeal to in the governed are unworthy and degrading. There are few common interests and no free play back and forth among the members of the group; stimulation and response are exceedingly one-sided. But if there is not a large variety of shared undertakings and experience in a social group, the influences that educate some into masters educate others into slaves. Dewey stressed particularly the fact that the arrest of free interchange of varying kinds of life experience results in a loss of meaning for the experience of *each* party. The evils affecting the superior class are less material and less perceptible, but equally real. "Their culture tends to be sterile, to be turned back to feed upon itself; their art becomes a showy display and artificial; their wealth luxurious; their knowledge overspecialized; their manners fastidious rather than humane."

Hence the exclusion of individuals or groups from any of the values of life they can enjoy not only limits and distorts those excluded but affects those who have excluded them; slavery affects slave-owners as well as slaves. By our treatment of minority groups today we lessen ourselves, create strains and stresses in our own personalities, rob ourselves of the contributions such groups could make to the common life, harm our inner equilibrium, and make ourselves intolerant, suspicious, fearful, and selfish. To realize the democratic ideal, we must make available to all the full range of the values our culture can provide. In educational terms, this means the schools must provide the opportunity to all to develop the capabilities and sensitivities necessary to enjoy and appreciate such values. Such an atmosphere provides one of the necessary conditions of creative activity.

Democracy, in Karl Popper's phrase, is an "open"

society. This means certainly that the arts are free from political interference, and that artists are free to create as their vision dictates. But it means more than that. Francis Villemain contrasts the conception of democracy as a catalog of specific goods to be obtained and as "a structure of ideas which releases and gives form to the process of moral reasoning and judgment." The "democratic ethical affirmation," he says, provides a format to "sustain the process of restating and enlarging goals and reconstructing the institutional and physical circumstances through which goals are brought into fruition." [17] This is to say that democracy is a process and that democratic ideals become the means by which we define—and under changing conditions, redefine—the quality of life we are to achieve. This process of definition and redefinition must, indeed, be within certain parameters—for example, the assumption of equality of opportunity, or the sanctity of the individual—that indicate the limits within which the discussion must be carried on. But within these parameters, the discussion is open-ended; no specific result is dictated by the form the discussion must take. This opens up the possibility of the perception and realization of new values, and precludes the imposition of extrinsic limitations on the values the artist can see and express and the opportunity of others to appreciate the new vision art can offer.

Most generally, it is democracy's interest in the opportunity each individual has for self-realization that creates a favorable environment for artistic creation and aesthetic appreciation. The harmonious development of all the individual's powers has been one of the themes in the philosophies of education developed under the influence of the democratic idea. For Pestalozzi the purpose of education was to be the training of the hand, the head, and the heart; the first of these included artistic skill as well as physical culture, and he urged that education of all three sides of our nature proceed on common lines in equal measure for the sake of the "unity of our nature and the equilibrium of our powers." One of the watchwords of education for Herbart was "many-sided interests"; education was to concern itself with all six types of interest that he found in human nature—empirical, speculative, and aesthetic knowledge, and sociality in its individual, civic, and religious aspects. Froebel likewise included art and objects of art as one of the major divisions of the curriculum, in this case again the aim being to secure full and all-sided development of each human being.[18]

In *School and Society*, Dewey included artistic expression among the human impulses that he regarded as "the natural resources, the uninvested capital, upon the exercise of which depends the active growth of the child." He believed aesthetic expression grew out of two other impulses, of communication and construction: "Make the construction adequate, make it full, free, and flexible, give it a social motive, something to tell, and you have a work of art." In his later and fuller discussion of education in a democracy, Dewey defined the prime function of literature, music, and the visual arts in education as the enhancement of the qualities that make any ordinary experience "appealing, appropriable—capable of full assimilation—and enjoyable." Although the fine arts, he said, are not the exclusive agency, they are the chief agencies of "an intensified, enhanced appreciation." They are both intrinsically and directly enjoyable, and serve the purpose of fixing taste and forming standards for the worth of later experiences. Thus they arouse discontent with conditions that do not measure up to their standards, and create a demand for improved surroundings. By revealing a depth and range of meaning in experiences that otherwise might be mediocre and trivial, they supply organs of vision. And in their fullness, "they represent the concentration and consummation of elements of good which are otherwise scattered and incomplete. They select and focus the elements of enjoyable worth which make any experience directly enjoyable. They are not luxuries of education, but emphatic expressions of that which makes any education worthwhile." [19]

The child's aesthetic and creative impulses were made central in the curriculum of the "progressive" schools that were created in the early part of this century, schools that have been attributed to Dewey's emphasis on the experience curriculum but that were also the product of the influence of expressionism in art.[20] In Rugg and Shumaker's survey of these "child-centered schools," much of which is devoted to an examination of the function of the various arts in their curriculum, the point is made that not only were the arts regarded as an invaluable part of the school program, but a new attitude toward art was taken. The emphasis was placed on "creative self-expression" or "creative originality in life," rather than upon the imposition of art and aesthetic standards upon the child. Every child was assumed to be endowed with the capacity to express himself, and this innate capacity was immensely worth cultivating. The pupil was placed in an atmosphere conducive to self-expression in every way. "The artist in Everyman's child is being discovered," Rugg and Shumaker claimed, "not only in the unusual, the gifted, the genius; the lid of restraint is being lifted from the child of the common man in order that he may come to his own best self-fulfillment." [21]

In summing up, however, Rugg and Shumaker criticized these schools for some of the same reasons Dewey was to give in *Experience and Education:* for the lack of continuity and real development in their programs and their failure to make systematic use of the techniques of science. Such schools came under even more serious attack by educational philosophers of a rationalist or realist persuasion, who saw nothing but disaster in an education based on self-expression untempered by rational discipline. The attempt to develop an educational philosophy that assigns to creativity its proper place in the curriculum may, as Hallman suggests,[22] be complicated by the fact that creativity itself involves both consciously controlled thought and unconscious mechanisms, craftsmanship and inspiration, the rational and predictable along with the irrational and unforeseen. Because of this, Hallman classifies philosophies of education into two groups, depending on which aspect of the creative act is found incompatible: those that stress the rational side of creativity—idealism and neo-Aristotelianism—and those that are concerned with the "immediacy of living—Zen Buddhism, existentialism, and psychotherapy. Because schooling has traditionally sided with the former philosophical orientation, Hallman believes it must, if it wishes to promote creativity, move in the direction of the more aesthetic systems. In general, this would mean that educators should take more seriously philosophies of process, of the Deweyan or Whiteheadian variety.

More recently, the attempt to develop a rationale for education based on the structure of knowledge [23] is a move in the direction of a curriculum, the balance of which is assured by a systematic analysis of the various modes of cognition. One of the forms this has taken has been the recent attempt of Phenix to develop a basis for the curriculum in the assumption that human beings are, essentially, creatures who can experience meanings, that distinctively human existence consists in a pattern of meanings, and that general education is the process of engendering essential meanings. Phenix finds six classes of meanings: symbolics, empirics, aesthetics, synectics, ethics, and synoptics; the task of education becomes that of an adequate representation of each of these in the curriculum of the school.[24]

It could be argued that, however favorable to the fine arts certain aspects of the democratic ideal may be, this healthy climate is largely canceled by the egalitarianism of democracy that creates an ethos within which excellence in the arts finds little response. For much of their history, the arts were the creatures of, and supported by, aristocracies, in part because only the aristocratic class possessed the leisure to enjoy the arts and acquire the sensibilities required for such enjoyment. The arts have been aristocratic also in the sense that they demand discrimination between the better and the worse, between excellence and shoddiness; as Dewey said, they create standards for measuring the worth of future experiences. Many have seen such values to be in direct contradiction to democratic egalitarianism, which they hold responsible for the "mass culture" attacked by such critics as Ortega y Gasset, T. S. Eliot, and Dwight MacDonald. Democracy exalts the "common man," and within 'such a society the mass of men determine taste. But according to a critic whose attitudes may be taken as typical:

> The mass of men dislikes and always has disliked learning and art. It wishes to be distracted from life rather than to have it revealed. It wishes to be comfortable in traditional and possibly happy and sentimental tropes, rather than to be upset by new

ones. It is true that it wishes to be thrilled, too. But irrational violence or vulgarity serves for that and for release, as sentimentality does for escape.[25]

False notions of equality may be responsible for a climate within which "superior culture," as Edward Shils calls it,[26] has great difficulty in maintaining itself, not to mention in flourishing. It seems more likely, however, that industrialism, including the development of mass communications, and the willingness of an amoral commercialism to exploit the feelings and aspirations of its audience for profit are more responsible than egalitarianism for the difficulties the arts face today. Shils is more optimistic about the position of the arts in a mass society than is Van den Haag, but to attempt to settle their dispute would require examination and evaluation of a vast and varied body of evidence. It is, however, worth noting that Shils attributes the troubles of the "superior" culture in this country in part to our universities, the strength of which lies not in liberal and undergraduate education but in a highly specialized postgraduate training that increasingly produces scientists, scholars, and technologists possessing only a narrow range of mediocre culture. This in turn is a response to our society's need for highly specialized skills, a need that finds expression in governmental support for the sciences and technology, thus effectively channeling the energies and talents of able students and faculty. Such tendencies can only be offset if we can formulate in a persuasive way the vital function performed by the arts in our national life. A. N. Whitehead, in his *Aims of Education,* summed up this function in impressive terms:

> The ultimate motive power, alike in science, in morality, and in religion, is the sense of value, the

38

sense of importance. It takes the various forms of wonder, of curiosity, of reverence, or worship, of tumultuous desire for merging personality in something beyond itself. This sense of value imposes on life incredible labours, and apart from it life sinks back into the passivity of its lower types. The most penetrating exhibition of this force is the sense of beauty, the aesthetic sense of realized perfection.[27]

References

1. Eliseo Vivas and Murray Krieger, *The Problems of Aesthetics* (New York: Holt, 1953), pp. 480–481.
2. Sidney Zink argues this position in detail in "The Moral Effect of Art," in Vivas and Krieger, *op. cit.,* pp. 553–554.
3. See, for example, Ephraim Vern Sayers and Ward Madden, *Education and the Democratic Faith* (New York: Appleton, 1959), p. 21. What Sayers and Madden call individualism corresponds to Lee's "sanctity of the self," which, along with "legitimacy of disbelief," Lee considers the central commitment of democracy. Gordon Lee, *Education and Democratic Ideals* (New York: Harcourt, 1965), pp. 11–16.
4. Francis Coker, *Recent Political Thought* (New York: Appleton, 1934), p. 372.
5. D. W. Gottschalk, *Art and the Social Order* (Chicago: University of Chicago Press, 1947), pp. 213–214.
6. John Dewey, *Art as Experience* (New York: Minton, Balch, 1934), p. 345.
7. George Santayana, *Life of Reason,* Vol. IV, *Reason in Art* (New York: Scribner's, 1937), p. 180.
8. *The New Yorker,* January 20, 1968, pp. 106–115.
9. Perhaps Arnstine's recent treatment of the aesthetic as the model for learning and education will foster a new trend in curriculum and methods of teaching. See Donald Arnstine, *Philosophy of Education: Learning*

THE ARTS IN HIGHER EDUCATION

and Schooling (New York: Harper, 1967), particularly Chapter 6, "Learning and Aesthetic Quality in Experience," and Chapter 7, "Practices of Schooling: The Aesthetic and Anesthetic."

10. Dewey, *op. cit.,* p. 348. Hence his remark, "As long as art is the beauty parlor of civilization, neither art nor civilization is secure." (*Ibid.,* p. 344.)

11. Philip Phenix, *Philosophy of Education* (New York: Holt, 1958), pp. 425–430.

12. Kenneth D. Benne, "Art Education as the Development of Human Resources," in *Art Education Today* (New York: Columbia University Press, 1948).

13. Ralph J. Hallman, "Creativity and Educational Philosophy," *Educational Theory, 17*:3–13 (January 1967).

14. Ralph J. Hallman, "The Commonness of Creativity," *Educational Theory, 13*:132–136 (April 1963). See particularly his discussion of Carl Rogers' concept of the therapeutic process.

15. See Paul R. Givens, "Creativity and the Gifted Child," *Educational Theory, 13*:129 (April 1963).

16. John Dewey, "The Democratic Conception in Education," *Democracy and Education* (New York: Macmillan, 1916).

17. Francis T. Villemain, "Democracy, Education, and Art," *Educational Theory, 14*:1–14, 30 (January 1964).

18. See Robert R. Rusk, *The Doctrines of the Great Educators* (New York: St. Martin's Press, 1965).

19. John Dewey, *Democracy and Education,* p. 238. See also Dewey's *Art as Experience,* particularly Chapter 3, "Having an Experience."

20. See Lawrence Cremin, *Transformation of the Schools* (New York: Knopf, 1962), pp. 201–207.

21. Harold Rugg and Ann Shumaker, *The Child-Centered School* (New York: World, 1928), p. 63.

22. Hallman, "Creativity and Educational Philosophy."

23. See, for example, Stanley Elam (Ed.), *Education and the Structure of Knowledge,* Fifth Annual Phi Delta Kappa Symposium on Educational Research (Chicago: Rand McNally, 1964).

24. Philip Phenix, *Realms of Meaning* (New York: McGraw-Hill, 1964).
25. Ernest Van den Haag, "A Dissent from the Consensual Society," in Hendrik M. Ruitenbeek (Ed.), *Varieties of Modern Social Theory* (New York: Dutton, 1963), p. 270.
26. As distinguished from "mediocre" and "brutal" culture. See Edward Shils, "Mass Society and Its Culture," in Ruitenbeek, *op. cit.,* pp. 232–258.
27. Alfred North Whitehead, *Aims of Education* (New York: Macmillan, 1959).

III

Albert Christ-Janer and Ralph L. Wickiser

Higher Education and the Arts

The arts ought to be important to all people, and consequently to all phases of education; the arts and other facets of higher education are interdependent and interrelated. Evaluation of the practice of the arts in higher education was made possible by the Land-Grant Act, with its emphasis on "Labor and Learning." The need for this evolution was foreseen by our founding fathers: "John Quincy Adams was prophetic indeed when he said that we must learn the arts of war and independence, so that our children can learn architecture and engineering, so that their grandchildren may learn Fine Arts and painting." [1]

However, it is a sad fact that throughout American history most educators have neglected the arts. An examination of the curriculum of the elementary school, the high school, and the college of the nineteenth century will show this to be true; in present-day school systems art is still uncomprehended and, consequently, undervalued. John A. Kouwenhoven measured the situation when he surveyed art in America in 1948. He wrote, "To many Americans the arts have always seemed to have little connection with our everyday life. . . . As a people we have been proud of American civilization and of its political and social institutions, but we have been less confident about our performance in the arts. . . . There are, for example, still relatively few institutions in our educational system where American art and literature are not regarded as mere appendages to other—and, on the whole, weightier —matters." [2]

While this condition has improved somewhat during the past two decades, the nonverbal arts are still not sufficiently appreciated in higher education. "Indeed, most universities have equated knowledge with the written word, saying in effect that human experience is recorded in books, professors write them, and students read them." [3]

This tendency to separate ideas and experience, to favor the written word, to value intellect above all else created the chasm between theory and practice. Xenophon said, "He who knows the theory but not the practice does not know the whole theory." [4] What, then, is the relation of theory to practice, and what does knowing the whole theory imply for art in higher education? "The antithesis between a technical and a liberal education is fallacious. There can be no adequate technical education which is not liberal, and no liberal education which is not technical; that is, no education which does not impart both technique and intellectual vision." [5] Some American philosophers and educators who tried to alter this trend, like John

Dewey, succeeded in changing the elementary school a great deal, the secondary school less, and higher education very little. Their attempts were largely aimed at reconciling the constructured paradox of theory versus practice. They brought art into the public schools and made it a forceful if not a required part of the curriculum.

The practical educator has been skeptical—and he still is—about the place art can have in an American educational program, but actually, art not only has a role in education; *art is education*. This basic fact has not been stressed frequently or vigorously enough.

What is generally known, for example, about the Greeks? What ties us to that mooring of ideas and forms? Mainly, the arts. The visual arts—the artistic monuments that stand today to represent their history; the sculptures that still reveal their culture; the frescoes and murals that now signify, as ever, the character of their time and place; the ceramics, jewelry, painted vases; the everlasting dramas of Sophocles and Euripides, which show us today the nature of their origins—all are, in themselves, education about man's best achievement. These are the most obvious sources of history, and consequently the most influential.

Yet the advocates of literary education regard the main link to be the word. This is so generally true in our land that we should ask, "How did we get so deeply into the habit of making so much out of the word?" The word is studied; someone believes every jot and tittle. Books about art monuments are held to be more authoritative than their subjects. Unending effort has gone into the study and interpretation of texts; we have trusted translations without questioning their sources; we have actually fought over a minute phrase or single word. And while the word has been so thoroughly our concern, the American educator has, by and large, neglected the direct

44

and meaningful message that might come from the object of art itself. Many educators have not seen enough of the Greek tragedies performed to appreciate their profounder meaning.

Who would be so foolish as to attempt to minimize the place of Socrates, Plato, and Aristotle; of Herodotus? No true educator would try to detract from these men who have, indeed, lighted up the ages. But a sophisticated teacher knows also that the works of the masters of the age of Pericles were hewn in eternal stone, etched in clay, and crystallized in dance and drama—they received the breath of life from the artist. He is fully aware that education is in the arts; that they are the source, that the desirable whole is the totality of all learning.

It is strange that the artist and the academician have been separated for so long. "The artist tries to express a universal truth through the particular whereas the scholar uses the particular as only a means of illustrating the universal." [6] Both are seeking truth in different ways with different means. Why, then, should it be difficult for them to understand each other? Works of art, as well as words, are instruments for communication. But it is communication made convincing through empathy, a mode of knowing that encompasses intellect, feeling, intuition, and man's other sensibilities. The arts, excepting poetry and the drama, of course, are essentially a nonverbal system that communicates more than the verbal abstraction. They are clothed with various kinds of sensibilities, including kinesthetic, and housed in a form through which the content is intuited. They are thus able to clarify and define ideas, often to make them more specific than words.

Meaning in architecture, the graphic and plastic arts, dance, and music starts where verbal communication leaves off. It defines specific and particular meanings of

45

ideas such as color, form, movement, and sound. These defy verbalization. In fact, if all dimensions of ideas could be expressed in words, all forms of communication could be verbal. But we know, for example, that the word "red," with all available adjectives, does not describe the infinite variety of ideas and feelings that the color red evokes in each of us. We know that ideas do not have to be verbalized to be expressed, and so painting, the dance, music, and sculpture exist to add their particular meaning to ideas.

There are many nonverbal systems besides painting and sculpture. Mathematics could not exist without symbols. Signs and symbols enter all phases of our daily life and thought. Acting is evidence that the spoken word is often insufficient to express the fullness of ideas. Music is a highly abstract nonverbal language, and most attempts to make music literal have failed. Music deals with ideas, and to watch a musician read and study a score reaffirms this. Musical ideas are not verbal, but they are ideas and they have a logic of their own. They demand internal consistency, continuity, and form to achieve their purpose. Thus, meaning in the arts is not the same as in other disciplines.

The attitude of too many academicians toward the arts has a long history. Suspicion of the arts did not begin in our time. As we know, current wisdom in ancient Greece considered art as skill [7] or as a mirror.[8] Art was considered poor philosophy, but philosophy excellent art.[9] The charm of art was thought to be dangerous, because it was pleasurable and a drain on reason.[10] Plato called the sculptor a common workman, not to be thought of as fine or noble or wise.[11] Plotinus considered the love of beauty to be metaphysical homesickness.[12] Medieval Christian thinkers thought art to be a liar who steals wholesome qualities from experience.[13] "Poets," they said, "are pernicious, for because of the sweetness of their modulations, souls fall from grace." [14]

Even the artists were cowed. Michelangelo, for instance, preferred not to be designated as a sculptor because that appellation classed him among the keepers of craft shops.[15] The Renaissance painters were constantly warned to be good men, well versed in literature.[16] The Renaissance artist was accorded the coveted title of philosopher only if he was as adept in divine wisdom as in natural wisdom. Leonardo, who obviously deserved the title, said that "Painting is philosophy because it subtly speculates on movement and form. The expressiveness and varieties of movement, and the truth of all natural species, seas and plains, trees, animals, plants and flowers, are her theme. And this is true knowledge." [17]

Leibniz's attitude toward art is typical of the schism that developed between art and philosophy in the "Age of Reason." In a letter he said, "I am sorry about the loss by fire of the Holbein paintings in Whitehall. Yet I feel after all a little like the Czar of Russia, who told me that he more admired certain pretty machines than all the beautiful paintings he had been shown in the King's palace." [18] Shelley wrote his "Defence of Poetry" in rebuttal to Sir Thomas Peacock's sneer at poetry as "a mental rattle and aimless mockery." [19] And evidence of jealousy is easily found in contemporary literature. Curt Ducasse wrote, "an artist with a theory should be regarded *a priori* with suspicion . . . it is something very different from dealing with theoretical questions concerning art when he is expert." [20]

Clinical evidence has been used to show that the artist creates out of rage. He uses creativity as a balm to heal "excess guilt, dread of the loss of love, and anxiety

47

over generative integrity which resulted from his latest explosion. As soon as he again considers his defense needs sufficiently threatened with thwarting, he will react with rage; and, cloistered once more in the grip of mobile depression, he will deliver himself from it eventually by moving through the cycle of suffering, free artistic invention, and the harmonious reclamation of human ties." [21] D. Bischler states that the artist selects certain mediums of expression because of fixation of a large amount of libido on erogenous zones. He finds fixation at the genital zone in all works of art. Fixation at the anal zone accounts for painters, sculptors, and decorators, while fixation at the oral zone accounts for musicians, poets, and other literary workers. Muscular eroticism accounts for dancers and similar performers. [22]

This quarrel needs to be stopped; it is unproductive, even harmful. The quarrel has separated two mutually dependent fields of knowledge, has supported the fallacious belief that the artist's hand is not at the disposal of an intellect. It posits that the faculty of knowing, the intellect, is devoid of feeling, intuition, and the forming function of art. It assumes that the acquisition of knowledge is the highest human virtue, and that knowledge is acquired solely through the intellect. Thus ideas and feelings have been separated. But inherently every idea has its equivalent in feeling, and feeling gives value to the idea. Without awareness of their felt context, ideas become inoperative. Without awareness of feeling reality becomes impersonal, unreal. Feeling makes ideas real, and therefore we must conclude that reality is richer than only spoken thought. The artist's mind operates in aesthetic situations rather than logical attitudes.

The aesthetic state of mind deals with wholes, and because of its process of synthesis it is difficult to enter and maintain. For this reason the import of the arts escapes most people. The arts appear to be esoteric, impractical, or superficial. But this can also be said of all complex processes that necessitate penetrating intellectual concentration or any prolonged creative effort demanding sustained attention. Thus, entering the aesthetic state of mind would seem to involve scholarship.

Scholarship in the arts is *achievement*. It is the development of visual and auditory ideas. All art criticism, history, theory or philosophy of art is knowledge about art; not art the process, but the creative act. If scholarship implies accurate and well-disciplined learning, then art activity makes full use of it. To illustrate, what could be more accurate than an organic spot of red on a canvas? This red is no statistical average red, it does not fluctuate with the laws of probability or chance; it is a precise red, the one and only red of its size, shape, time, and space. And who, we might ask, is more disciplined than the musician who composes a concerto, or the sculptor who carves a large mass of marble into exquisite shapes?

Great artistic ideas, unlike scientific ideas, are not outmoded by new achievements. These art activities require severe intellectual discipline, a vigorous disenchantment with accepted concepts. But the *practice* of art is more than an intellectual discipline. The discipline of the intellectual virtues, through formal and rigorous exercises upon difficult and exacting material, leaves little room for the pursuit of qualities the artist cherishes. The artist is not as interested in knowing as he is in forming. To the philosopher an image implies the representation of an object, the sign signifies it. The artist must acquire knowledge as a means to form his experience. It is a means for him, not an end. "Art is the representation, science the explanation—of the same reality." [23]

The arts and philosophy as well as the natural and social sciences have much in common to those people seeking the common core of cultural concepts. Ultimately everyone is searching for the meaning of reality within his chosen medium. All are interested in the problem of knowledge in its larger sense as it becomes wisdom. The arts, through their concern for feeling, are the logical counterpart of philosophy and its concern with thought. Without either one, experience loses its synthesis and there is a dilemma in the halls of learning.

Ideally, no place is better suited to solve this dilemma than the liberal arts college. But the college must be forced to reckon with the present as well as the past, with imagination as well as intellect, with action as well as contemplation—that is, action as it pertains to the arts, because these activities involve contemplation while some activity is not contemplative. But activity *is* integral to the arts.

The artist is judged by the work he produces, not by his theories or intentions. As Focillon says, "The mind rules over the hand; hand rules over mind. The gesture that makes nothing, the gesture with no tomorrow, provokes and defines only the state of consciousness. The creative gesture exercises a continuous influence over the inner life. The hand wrenches the sense of touch away from its merely receptive passivity and organizes it for experiment and action. It teaches man to conquer space, weight, density, and quantity. Because it fashions a new world, it leaves its imprint everywhere upon it. It struggles with the very substance it metamorphoses and with the *very form* it transfigures." [24]

The artist must see his role in higher education. The arts, as creative activity, must be reevaluated in the light of modern scientific learning so that we can see how

50

imperative they are to man's emotional maturity, how they function in mental health, in biophysical development, in the growth of personality. Where else in the curriculum will the student be trained in feeling, in the integration of thought and feeling, in emotional maturity, in the relation of theory to practice?

We need to understand the arts as evolving activities and not become dismayed by their changing nature, by the loss of security they sometimes reveal. We must not fall back on blind disciplines because they offered us security in the past. We must overcome our fear of unleashing the creative imagination in the present. With Leonardo we must realize that "All knowledge originates in our sensibilities." [25] Education should use "the artist's intuition which will serve as the most gracious and far-sighted guide, because it performs the synthesizing function in the human constitution, and puts sense, mind, and spirit into the wholes which it produces. . . ." [26]

We need the wholly educated teacher who has been exposed constantly to all of the meritorious works of mankind. There is no excuse for anyone devoted to education to say, "I know my history, literature, my science—but I don't know anything about art." All too often this is stated with even a show of pride. It is, rather, a shameful confession, and the need for it could be eliminated through a broader and more richly rewarding application.

In spite of many attempts to include some aspects of the arts in general education, most college students receive little excellent formal education in the arts. During the postwar years much has been said and written about the value of the liberal arts, as if this value had only just been discovered. A good part of this argument is specious.

The position so frequently taken is that all students

will be best served by a curriculum of required subjects which, offered formally and usually by lectures, can remove cultural inadequacies. Of course the benefits of broadening liberal studies have been recognized through the centuries. But there is ample proof that the required program of diversification in our present-day basic education in colleges and universities may produce the dilettante; even worse, and where the waste is insupportable, the talented student with powerful motivation often gets involved in inert ideas and disjointed thoughts from desultory course material, and loses his original interest. With his central purpose forgotten, with his interest dissipated in years of slave labor in courses, the student's ambitions fade. His vision fails. What should be the quest for a liberal education ends for many by being only a floundering in generalities—a condition that Alexander Pope warned is cultural tragedy.

In addition to this frustration of the student's ambition, those not frustrated are still not as well educated as they could be with a curriculum designed to educate all of their abilities, sensibilities, and interests. Therefore, in our domestic system a variety of educational programs should be offered to the variety of talents we must educate and train. A selection of programs is possible that will adequately supply the need of those students who, at an early age, know what they want and want to know how to do it.

Only pedants scorn a useful education, as Alfred North Whitehead so sensibly pointed out about thirty-five years ago, when he asked, "If an education is not useful, what is it?" What prompts us, heirs of the influential professional studies of the ancient curricula of the universities of Bologna and Paris, to question the merit of usable knowledge? We have been misled about Platonism by some who, like Robert Maynard Hutchins, had only the best of intentions in attempting to purge trivia from the curriculum. Sadly, all too often the "pure" liberal arts studies have become a dodge for the basically uninterested who are driven by social urges to join the fraternity of wanderers; worse than this, a few, originally talented and self-directed, have lost their way in the first years of floundering in college and university "liberalizing" programs.

All this is not to say, of course, that only that subject matter which can be immediately applied is important; this would be a naïve and harmful misconception. It must be realized that depth perception is also an outgoing view; or, as Arthur Pope used to say, "by searching downward into the matter, the student will be forced to look outward also." For example, a design student with an inquisitive mind and professional ambitions might become engrossed in the notebooks of Leonardo da Vinci. Here he would discover ideas that would interest him because of his central obsession with invention and form. A penetrating study of this Renaissance master would, naturally, plunge the student into sixteenth century Italy; he would be motivated to read extensively in the history of that fascinating time. This might lead him, as so many have been led, into an absorbing study of history. Thus the cultured mind develops; he will be urged into learning for learning's sake, in addition to his concern for utility. What an attractive paradox! For this goal is that of the most ardent proponent of the "pure" liberal arts studies.

A clear course can be charted, certainly, between the Scylla of desultory, required studies so often foisted on students and the Charybdis of strict, unimaginative technology that has turned out some very dull technicians. A better program can be visualized and a curriculum can emerge that combines doing and thinking, that unites in one personality the ideal of Plato and of St. Benedict. The works of the Benedictines are blessed by the spirit of disinterested curiosity central to the Platonist's aim. Thus, in its essence, to quote Whitehead again, "A liberal education is an education for thought and for aesthetic appreciation. It proceeds by imparting a knowledge of the masterpieces of thought, of imaginative literature, and of art." Then art itself, as we proposed at the beginning of this discussion, is the wellspring. And from it the real student will "drink deep, or taste not the Pierian spring."

Surely the professional arts can deepen and complement liberal arts studies. For example, history departments can enrich their offerings by seeking the aid of the art historian. Students of English literature find William Blake more meaningful and complete if they study his drawings. Chippendale's work can shed light on the eighteenth century if it is carefully examined and its eclectic quality analyzed. A harvest scene by "Peasant" Breughel can intimately show rural Flemish life of the Reformation period. Michelangelo and Bernini can reveal, through St. Peter's facade and piazza, the grandeur of that church at its most brilliant time. The temple of Luxor can light up the Egyptian dynasties with a clarity that radiates from no word.

We are bound then, to enrich the liberal arts studies by digging deep into the rich ore of art itself, and to deepen the arts by relating them to the liberal arts offerings. Thus, the schools or departments of art can profit from a more scholarly pursuit of history of the arts. They should urge the students who need languages to take the necessary courses. Studio work in the arts, like laboratory work in the sciences, can complement the material offered in the lecture room. The word and the deed together make up the ideal program; their union brings greater depth to the liberal arts studies and new dimensions to the professional art programs.

In addition to this rounding out of the liberal arts student's education, the arts offer some very specific educational experiences not found in book learning that often prove crucial in his ability to act with feeling and wisdom. To know the full value of art in higher education, then, we must examine the arts as active knowledge.

The art act is essentially a creative search to establish the questions that form the myths of our time. It involves the total person with all his sensibility, his kinesthetic control, his intuition, insight, apprehension, intelligence, and many other facets of which we are unaware. We might symbolize the artist's action as a circle divided into many parts, only one part being verbal intelligence. Thus, thinking about art, however important, is only a small part of the total act. The arts, as disciplines, have many things in common with other disciplines. They deal with ideas and problem-solving. They attempt a synthesis of knowledge based on learned information. They employ logic when necessary and search for value judgments based on universal truths. But the basic difference between the arts and other disciplines is creative imagination.

The primary role of the arts in higher education, then, must be predicated on the ulterior purpose of developing each person's creative imagination fully through the creation of art works or the enjoyment of art experiences. It should also encompass each person's real need for achieving aesthetic maturity, to ensure the maximum development of all his abilities, mental, physical, emotional, and spiritual. The philosophical basis for the arts in higher education deals with the value import of the aesthetic experience as educative material. Our primary values, ethical, moral, and aesthetic, are implicit in qualitative experience and influence all judgments. These values are mutually dependent in many ways, but the desire to isolate aesthetics from religion has created an overemphasis on the isolation and singularity of the aesthetic experience as a value factor. Although this isolation made possible the idea that art is self-justifying, all value judgments involve aesthetic factors. However, we must not overemphasize the preciousness of aesthetic values, for, in reality, each person uses them in all his value judgments. In a larger sense, art is purposive as well as nonpurposive. All people search for aesthetic values to guide their decisions; even though most people are not aware of it, they are intimately concerned with values involving aesthetic judgments.

The arts offer the student an opportunity to discover personally the significance of qualitative experience through creative imagination. They are a last refuge of idealism in modern education. If quality is to continue in society schools must create it, in spite of the tremendous onslaught of mass culture and the overemphasis on quantitative experiences that dominate the curriculum. Quantitative experience can be logically arranged to appeal to materialistic beliefs. A premium is placed on logical processes of learning that emphasize the ability to think as the primary requisite of an educated man, largely eliminating what he thinks about. The arts in higher education can and must avoid this pitfall. They must point the way to an educative process that ensures each person's total maturity by developing his creative imagination.

Education in the arts should then be based on a clear understanding of the nature of art, the creative processes, and creative imagination. To make maximum use of the creative imagination, it is necessary to recognize two fundamental social concepts of the artist. We must have first a concept of "man as artist," and second, a concept of "artist as man," as a creative person whose importance to society is felt and recognized. If we examine the concept of "man as artist" we discover that all people have the art impulse—they yearn to commune and share with others. The arts are not merely communication, as most people think. They are not the transfer of ideas but the sharing of aesthetic experiences. Man needs order to make his life more meaningful, beauty to lift him out of the realms of drabness, and expression to fix permanently his moments of ecstasy. In like manner, the concept of "artist as man" presumes he is a creative force in society. This concept has been constructed and romanticized in our folklore to the point where the artist is characterized as a psychological misfit; even he often believes it. A new concept of the "artist as man" must therefore replace this outdated notion, especially in education.

If both aspects of the artist's function in society were considered, a program could be built that would meet the aesthetic needs of all students since it would be basic to everyone's creative development. The creative imagination that defies outworn convention, that breaks down pseudo ideas and beliefs, that inner force which leads to self-criticism and a constant search for self-improvement—can be kindled in everyone. We must assume, with Dewey, that all people can develop their creative imagination to varying degrees and develop the skills adequately to express themselves; that everyone can become interested in aesthetic experience through participation in a creative process.

If the arts and the other disciplines are to become indispensable partners in fact, an educational program should be developed that allows this partnership to benefit all, not merely the interested few who have predilections for the arts. The very real possibility of discovering the talents of many students in the complex university or the liberal arts college is challenging—so many latent abilities may there be unearthed.

On the one hand, the artists must learn about verification as well as creativity, logic as well as feeling. In turn, their associates in the colleges should learn to participate in various art experiences with knowledge and understanding through practice. They should learn thereby to date, to discover, to feel, to ridicule, and to praise; to blaspheme and to love. Through action they may learn the logic and structure of feeling. And together, all the students may realize that many works of distinction are the results of thoughts that are not literal. Then, to paraphrase Harold Taylor, the arts are education and education itself becomes an art.

References

1. J. A. Perkins, "University and the Arts," *Teachers College Record,* 66:671 (May 1965).
2. John A. Kouwenhoven, *Made in America* (New York: Doubleday, 1949).
3. Perkins, *op. cit.,* p. 675.
4. *Ibid.,* p. 676.
5. Alfred North Whitehead, *The Aims of Education* (New York: New American Library, 1948), p. 58.
6. Perkins, *op. cit.,* p. 675.
7. Quoted by Katharine Gilbert and Helmut Kuhn, *A History of Aesthetics* (New York: Macmillan, 1953), p. 19.
8. *Ibid.,* p. 28.
9. *Ibid.,* p. 55.
10. *Ibid.,* p. 37.
11. *Ibid.,* p. 56.

12. *Ibid.*, p. 112.
13. *Ibid.*, p. 122.
14. *Ibid.*, p. 123; quoted from Lactantius.
15. Quoted by Gilbert and Kuhn, *op. cit.*, pp. 203–204.
16. *Ibid.*, p. 173.
17. Edward MacCurdy (Ed.), *The Notebooks of Leonardo da Vinci*, Vol. II (New York: Reynal, 1939), p. 228.
18. Quoted by Gilbert and Kuhn, *op. cit.*, pp. 203–204.
19. *Ibid.*, p. 405.
20. C. J. Ducasse, *The Philosophy of Art* (New York: Dial Press, 1929), p. 2.
21. Harry B. Lee, "A Theory Concerning Free Creation in the Inventive Arts," *Psychiatry: Journal of the Biology and Pathology of Interpersonal Relations*, 3:293 (May 1940).
22. *Ibid.*, p. 254.
23. Herbert Read, *Education Through Art* (New York: Pantheon, 1958), p. 11.
24. Henri Focillon, *The Life of Forms in Art* (New York: Wittenborn, 1958).
25. MacCurdy, *op. cit.*, p. 67.
26. Edward F. Rothschild, *The Meaning of Unintelligibility in Modern Art* (Chicago: University of Chicago Press, 1934), p. 6.

IV

Edward L. Mattil

Teaching the Arts

How and where the arts are learned may be of greater significance than how successfully they are taught. The arts are learned in university lecture halls and in small hallways, at concerts and through the hi-fi, in the gallery and on the street, in crowds and in isolation, and the learning may be carefully structured and formal or casual and accidental. The arts are taught by teachers who enjoy students and who find teaching a rewarding, creative delight, and by teachers who find teaching a dull, interfering bore and think of students as the enemy.

It is difficult to determine when or if the marriage of the fine arts and the university took place, but at least there is a record of a long courtship as evidence of their intentions. Some college and university people feel that the arts have been thrust on them and there remains no choice but to accept that hairy mantle. Although the courtship was long, not until the arts moved into the house

60

did the real problems of living together have to be faced and solved.

There are some who feel that to include the arts, especially those areas of fine arts education having to do with the training of professionals, in higher education is a mistake. This issue has been widely aired, and it is now generally agreed that the arts are solidly entrenched in higher education.

For many years the fine arts have been relegated to a position of secondary importance in the academic world, as well as in the world at large. This station is changing somewhat as higher education increasingly responds to what students and the public feel is a real need. Higher education usually does more than just respond. It recognizes and encourages the thrusts and currents of the external world and, in time, finds the means of bringing important movements into the academic fold. Thus, the "cultural explosion" has made the extensive inclusion of the arts a legitimate concern of higher education. But this inclusion has not been without its problems. The arts, frequently nonverbal and affective in their approaches, have moved into a climate traditionally dominated by conceptual approaches to learning that rely on verbalization as almost the sole method of communication. The arts bring faculties who are relatively unfamiliar and unconcerned with the expectations of colleges and universities face to face with scholars of another tradition. How well traditional university faculties can accept the artists and how well the artists can endure the conditions of university life are questions essentially unanswered. Some feelings of perhaps both skepticism and hostility exist that I am confident can be resolved when all the elements have been arranged for greater harmony.

Higher education appears to be seeking ways to

add the dimensions of seeing, hearing, and feeling to the education of students. As natural avenues to greater sensibility and sensitivity, the fine arts are abundantly favorable for this purpose. College students are literate in the traditional sense, but higher education historically has paid little attention to developing visual or auditory literacy. The abundance of visual and auditory ugliness testifies to that neglect. A five-mile stretch of road on the outskirts of any community reveals how creeping ugliness takes over when the population is insensitive, unaware, and unprepared to cope with it. The most influential segment of our population, the college-educated, has essentially been overlooked in visual and auditory education.

Now colleges and universities are including in their curricula the methods and materials of the musician, actor, potter, painter, poet, and dancer as byways to aesthetic and creative experiences. These experiences are not only educationally valuable to students, but also give them opportunities for self-renewal that modern life with its many barriers seems so determined to stamp out. No one believes the arts to be the only avenues to creative and aesthetic growth, but the fine arts are uniquely suited to evoke strong responses in both the naïve and the sophisticated. And since colleges and universities enroll both extremes, they are meeting their responsibilities to both groups through the fine arts.

The history of the fine arts in education reveals the extent to which a variety of institutions have for many years incorporated the arts into their programs. Some of today's campus "innovations" have been quietly practiced for many years. Robert Frost was a resident poet more than four decades ago. Bennington, Smith, the University of Wisconsin, and other institutions have continuously and successfully engaged artists-in-residence. Nor is the serious involvement of art as part of the curriculum a recent development. Bennington, for example, has for more than thirty years successfully integrated the arts into a serious academic curriculum and has reported positive effects upon the whole learning process in the entire curriculum.

The question of whether or not the arts should be part of higher education has for all purposes been substantially answered, and the real questions are how the fine arts can be taught effectively and for what ends. History provides only a few landmark efforts as guides. To look at the entire problem in less general terms, eight subquestions will be considered.

Is higher education willing to accept the fine arts, particularly those aspects concerned with professional training? Many levels of acceptance are required. One of the most obvious depends upon the willingness of administrators to pay for an expensive new component that is largely untried and that has not been generally recognized as a "useful" subject. Present evidence suggests that to a high degree acceptance at this level already has been achieved. The abundance of new theaters, studio art buildings, auditoriums, and music buildings testifies to the willingness of taxpayers, trustees, and donors to pay for the fine arts.

Clearly the pressure of leisure time and its effective use have caused university leaders to begin to prepare to meet these needs. Why the university? Frankly, as with many another modern dilemma, there was nowhere else to refer the problem. College and university administrators, we are told, ultimately consider every problem and request that has no established organization for its solution. That the arts problem was not rejected was due to several factors. To begin with, there is a history of some success in higher education; this foothold consisted of a nucleus of arts staffs and buildings on many campuses. Second, colleges and universities have learned to serve their students and the public by sharing talent and resources. The newer co-operative arrangements such as those implemented by arts councils and community art centers as well as community-shared resident musical and theater groups make possible endeavors that single institutions might otherwise be unwilling or unable to attempt alone. A typical example is the arts festival involving many independent art groups and institutions along with the college or university. We conclude that college administrators have, for the most part, provided support and interest for the arts on campus.

Another level of acceptance depends on the crucial reactions of existing faculties. Popular interest in the arts is unlikely to generate the same enthusiasm from those who are the guardians of tradition, those who distinguish between scholars and others, and especially those who stand at the portals of the graduate faculty. In spite of the fact that some problems are to be expected, universities are no strangers to problems; therefore with time tradition will bend and the new elements will find the acceptance necessary for survival.

Still another acceptance must come from the artist, who undoubtedly will find life in a college environment different and perhaps obstructively demanding. Every institution makes demands, their gentleness notwithstanding. Frequently the artist is called upon for the unscheduled and unpredictable, resulting from the spontaneous needs of students or the institution. As a result it is difficult, if not impossible, to describe accurately to the prospective artist-teacher or artist-in-residence what his role will be. However, more and more of America's artists of significance are somewhat familiar with higher education. Over

90 per cent of them have prepared in colleges and art schools, but a recent study by Michaels [1] reported that only about half of them felt that their art training was of value. This suggests that not all the artists being hired by colleges and universities will believe in the system they are entering.

Another problem of acceptance concerns higher education's ability to find ways to admit students whose interests and achievements do not match the institution's broadest admission requirements. This is a complex problem not likely to be solved by being idealistic or by pressing the virtues of creativeness, talent, or other potentials. Until there is a substantial body of evidence to the contrary, students who show little promise of being able to achieve satisfactorily in typical course work are unlikely to be admitted. Many people fear that present standards may be keeping highly creative, talented students out of colleges and universities. A recent study by Getzels and Czikszentmihaly [2] pointed out significant differences, particularly in value orientation and personality characteristics, between art students and non-art students in degree-granting institutions. The extent to which these and other differences affect admission warrants considerable investigation if talent and creativeness are not to be bypassed. My own impression is that although creativeness is not used as a criterion for selection or admission, creative students are not being rejected; but this problem cannot be handled by guesses or intuition.

What bearing does the cultural explosion have on education in the fine arts? Sometime during the present decade the term "'cultural explosion" was coined, and for the past half dozen years it has been the subject of much discussion. At first, remarkedly few data were available to chart just what was happening. Then several extensive studies—such as the Rockefeller Panel Report on the

Performing Arts [3]—began to clarify the picture. As reported in this study, an enormous expansion has taken place in the fine arts. Recently, an entire issue of *Look* magazine devoted to the "Sound and Fury in the Arts" focused on the new generation of artists, the mushrooming metropolitan art centers, and the "culture happy" communities of America. It described Americans as "concert-going, book-talking, and art-buying," armed with affluence and leisure—an audience that might be spending $7 billion annually by the 1970's on everything from recordings to Renoirs.[4] According to the Rockefeller Report, in 1965 there were 1401 symphony orchestras in the country, as contrasted with about 700 in 1939. The number of opera companies has grown to 754, double the number of a decade earlier. Presently there are about 40,000 separate theatrical enterprises, representing an increase of 15 per cent in a period of ten years. There were about 200 dance companies in 1965.[5]

The creation of the National Foundation on the Arts and the Humanities in 1965 doubtlessly will ensure a steady increase in the fine arts, resulting from the hope of new financial support from the federal government. (The 1967–68 appropriation for the Foundation amounts to approximately $14 million. This is several million dollars less than the cost of the lunar test vehicle that performed briefly, although not entirely successfully, for a small audience recently and was then abandoned to drift in space or burn up.)

An alarming fact brought out by the Rockefeller Report is that almost all growth reported is amateur. The picture of the professional artist remains a dismal one, although audience receptiveness for both the performing and the plastic arts has never been better. Theaters are full, concerts are well attended, and museums are staggered

66

by the impressive attendance and the use of their re-sources. However, in spite of the general receptivity of audiences, economic factors work against the artist, keep-ing him only one step away from poverty. Naturally, the "stars" are excepted from this generalization, but the data on symphony musicians, on artists who do not have "name" galleries behind them, and on actors who are bringing live theater to local audiences are depressing.

Two major concerns resulting from this growth in the arts confront higher education. The first is finding means to provide financial help for the artists, by using their works as well as by employing some of them within the university community. A second concern is recognizing that the cultural explosion could lower overall quality in the arts. There is no doubt that the practice of democracy can pose a threat to that quality. Television ratings indi-cate the level to be expected when popular choice is the criterion. On the basis of an unselected or "popular" audi-ence, we have to accept the fact that the wider the audience, the lower the common denominator. According to one recent newspaper story, students still prefer a performance by Jefferson Airplane to one by a symphony orchestra or a classical musician. Students apparently can enjoy a wide range of artists, from "pop" to classical, and the range of tastes requires respect, even admiration, from those who program for audience-building and audience-educating.

Whether or not students are supporting art, "cul-tural ooze," or "kitsch," they want to support culture and art on their campuses and think they are doing so. Mass efforts in the arts need not necessarily produce mediocre results. There is an eager, receptive audience that wants to learn, but helping them learn requires a serious, long-term, and sustained effort in audience-building and audi-ence education. This is an essential responsibility for

67

higher education. Colleges and universities are the places most able to insist on quality and, as national cultural leaders, to help determine standards.

Do the fine arts provide an essential balance to the heavy emphasis on science and technology? Some of the most impressive arguments for balance have come from scientific leaders who have urged a partnership of the sciences, humanities, and the arts. Glenn T. Seaborg, chairman of the U.S. Atomic Energy Commission, when appearing before the Senate Special Subcommittee on the Arts and Humanities, pointed out what he considered to be a major imbalance in our national personality in regard to the place of science.[6] He called for a learning balance in both formal and continuing education, and stressed the need for supporting students and institutions concerned with the arts and humanities. Mr. Seaborg specifically called attention to those aspects of the humanities, the creative arts, which in themselves constitute values. Music, dance, drama, and art all hold values that are ends in themselves and at the same time offer rewards in terms of our pursuit of happiness. Mr. Seaborg and other scientists believe that many facets of the arts and humanities can stimulate the creative aspects of science and technology— aspects that tend to broaden the imagination and expand the aims and goals. The experiences of Gyorgy Kepes and Robert Preusser in teaching visual design to science and engineering students at Massachusetts Institute of Technology illustrate the possibility of releasing large, untapped potentials for visual thinking and artistic imagination in people whose professions have no direct relationship to or contact with the visual arts.[7]

Mr. Seaborg also called for attention to leisure time, stressing that the spiritual, physical, and mental well-being of our population is critical. He argued that while leisure is increasing, few people are prepared to use it effectively.

The arts phenomenon of the 1960's may be serving as a barometer of a serious human need. What is happening is difficult to comprehend. New music, radically new plastic art forms, new dance, multimedia "happenings" appear, then disappear rapidly, but the movement continues energetically—sometimes almost frantically—and search and experimentation continue among artists. Even or perhaps especially among non-artists there is eagerness to participate in the arts dialogue. The arts education of youth has surely spurred this interest. Higher education, in providing the opportunity to continue these experiences, is supporting the premise that the arts do make people more sensitive, more perceptive, more appreciative, more creative, and more knowledgeable.

Each of the arts is an assembly, a storehouse of opportunities, of aesthetic and creative objects and experiences. The arts are available, they exist in profusion, they can be observed and studied, and they are to some extent teachable. The university is uniquely suited to provide conditions that create a healthy educational balance between the sciences, the arts, and the humanities. To a large extent, this is the present trend.

To what extent are the colleges and universities encouraging and engaging in support for the performing arts? Recently the *New York Times* featured a survey on live entertainment on the campus. It reported that more than 70 per cent of the concert activity of professional artists can be attributed to the college market. Colleges are the largest buyers and consumers of serious music, and last year spent about $40 million on pop concerts.[8] This is not new, for some schools have long been offering concert experiences to their students. This past year, the

University of Michigan included seven foreign symphony orchestras in its eighty-ninth concert season. Although good music is at home on the campus, this dramatic increase has created a market that makes colleges and universities the twentieth century chief patrons of the arts.

According to the Association of College and University Concert Managers, much of the supporting money for these programs comes from university operating funds, some from student-body fees, and some from admissions charges. Performers' fees have made sizable gains, with pop groups like the Supremes commanding higher fees than Serkin, Rubinstein, and other classical musicians. The extent of campus concert interest is reflected in the number of colleges represented by the Association of College and University Concert Managers. In 1957 they represented thirty-five campuses, today 375.[9]

In spite of these impressive figures, some schools report that many concerts are poorly attended even though tickets are distributed free. As a result, nonstudents have been allowed to buy tickets. This should be a first step in a long-range, planned program in sharing. As new concert halls are built, as resident quarters are engaged, as expensive electronic equipment is acquired, some means of sharing both the use and the expense of these facilities should be considered. Few institutions can afford the luxury of resources that are only half used. Even if auditoriums become rehearsal halls, lecture halls, and examination centers, these secondary uses often reflect poor planning.

The university needs to study its position in shared responsibility in relation to other institutions and groups and consider its special resources and capabilities—its staff, equipment, and buildings. More importantly, it must determine its leadership responsibilities. Through the creation of the many state arts councils, higher education's

70

special obligations and those areas that it might wisely abandon can now be more easily identified. The need for being a solitary leader has markedly diminished. Higher education must decide what it can do best, especially in those activities that other groups will not or cannot support and develop. To try to be all things to all people is foolhardy and guaranteed to ensure a drop in the quality level.

What can the university contribute to the training of professionals in the fine arts? This issue has many ramifications and few areas of wide agreement. W. McNeil Lowry of the Ford Foundation, in an address to the Association of Graduate Schools in 1961, said, "Under present conditions the best service you can perform for the potential artist is to throw him out." [10] This remark could not be interpreted as facetious, for it followed a carefully conceived discussion of the creative arts in the university. The advice, however, cannot be easily accepted. Mr. Lowry would concede that because of the extent of the present commitment, the trend is unlikely to be reversed. This trend resulted in part from the fact that the few institutions engaged solely in the preparation of artists could not continue to carry the entire burden. Indeed, many of them have already broadened their programs to become more like colleges, and through a variety of arrangements are now degree-granting institutions.

What does it mean to teach artists? There is some general agreement that art can be taught (although no one is absolutely sure what art is) in diverse ways—through its history, processes, media, appreciation, and forms. But teaching artists is another matter, since there is little agreement on what constitutes an artist's education. Michaels' study of living American artists [11] reported that the majority are concerned with society in general and with what is going on in the world. More than half of those

71

questioned felt that art programs are influential and needed in professional development. Since 96 per cent of today's artists have had formal training in a college or an art school, this is one route.

To teach artists first implies that there are people who want, above all things, to become artists, and that these individuals can get into an institution where training is available. It also implies the availability of teachers, studios, art works, and libraries. The problem of teaching artists today is complicated by the fact that no one can say for sure what art is or what form it should take. In the past artists were trained "in the tradition," but what is today's tradition? Therefore, training artists amounts to directing the attention of prospective artists to the study and practice of their art through the study of mankind and of significant artists and their products, and through the creation of works of art.

To offer professional training on the campus will require more artists as teachers and artists-in-residence. To use artists on campus successfully requires finding out what each individual can contribute, and how. A role cannot be predetermined; rather, it must be developed. The problem must be viewed from the vantage points of both the university and the artist. What can each contribute to the other? If arrangements between artist and university are primarily economic—that is, so many dollars for so many musical compositions or paintings—the project will undoubtedly not succeed. Such a project will attract the wrong sort of artist—the hungry and the exploitable. The university must provide an enhancing environment that will nourish and encourage the artist's professional development and his professional career. In return, the artist's presence must augment and enrich the university's

72

resources and climate, steadily offering contributions outside of regular curricular patterns.

Blind faith in a balanced exchange between the university and the artist is not enough. Some artists are suited to such an agreement, others not, regardless of their solid professional reputations. It is essential to select those who have a genuine interest in the relationship and who do not object to guiding others and sharing some time with them. Some colleges and universities are suited to apply such arrangements advantageously; others have not yet achieved the climate in which both the student and the artist-teacher can benefit from the association. Artists want to be neither missionaries nor subjects of dilettantes' interest. But in spite of the high risk factors, the preparation of professionals is possible, and colleges and universities are indeed the most fertile seed beds for new talent.

Are the fine arts teachable? An abundance of objects, practices, media, and history exists for each of the fine arts. There are examples of good practices for the teaching of the arts, for the preparation of teachers, and for the development of teaching materials. Except for the requirements for certification or accreditation, there is little to suggest uniformity.

A major problem is the ability of those who determine curriculum and those who teach to distinguish among the numerous goals for the teaching of art. What shall be taught and how depends entirely upon the populations to be taught and the purposes for teaching them. The novice cannot be taught in the same way as the sophisticate, nor can the potential artist be taught in the same way as the potential audience. Nor, by the same token, can all teachers reach all students with equal success. As an illustration of this problem, in a study entitled

73

The Visual Arts in Higher Education,[12] the so-called "bread and butter" courses of art history departments were reported as offering little glory, and "to the scholar they are often a drudgery and distraction." The largest and probably most important courses are assigned to the least distinguished and experienced members of the faculties, and "as a result, many of them are poorly taught." This report injects an interesting but highly questionable thought when it suggests that the really able student will not be deterred by a "wretched introductory course or by a boring survey. If he has the stamina to suffer through them, he is likely to persevere to the end." (What the art historians have reported frankly and honestly is undoubtedly a criticism that might be leveled at many fields of study and their faculties.)

This study does underline a critical need. If the arts are to be taught effectively to growing numbers of students with widely differing needs and levels of ability, a wider range of types of teachers is required. Scholars and artists who are uninterested or who dislike teaching should not be used to alienate those who have a thirst for art, be it ever so small.

There has been a tendency to pay little attention to the preparation of teachers of art for higher education. That *The Visual Arts in Higher Education* devotes so much space to pointing out the weaknesses of teaching in the secondary schools is reminiscent of Mark Twain's remark, "Nothing so needs reforming as other people's habits." Science and engineering are paying greater attention to the preparation of collegiate teachers, while the arts have largely neglected this problem by assuming that scholarly or artistic competence automatically qualifies a person to teach.

An immediate requirement is the willingness to

recognize that education in the arts assumes many forms and has many goals. Although marked differences in forms and purposes are apparent, these differences should never be used as measures of importance. It must be understood that students at any institution can be grouped into different levels of talent, interest, or sophistication in relation to their separate purposes and goals in the arts. Thus grouped, they should progress educationally toward their separate goals. Although it is a matter of judgment, it appears that the strongest programs exist where there is some means of separating and identifying staffs according to their functions. This reduces the problem of hierarchies and allows each teacher to focus on the importance of his own sphere of interest and influence.

Are the colleges and universities responsible for preparing audiences for the fine arts? Formal required experiences in the fine arts generally end at the junior high school or middle school level. After this period, arts education depends upon self-education or an occasional course. Studies of the arts programs in elementary schools reveal that only about 10 per cent of the arts education of children has been handled by teachers qualified or prepared to teach the arts.[13] If the growing audiences for the arts are to follow their interests, they will need greater help, particularly if as audiences they are to affect positively the directions of the arts. The universities are slowly moving from a position of casual, fashionable interest to one of serious, planned commitment. Without clearly defined goals and planned implementation, programs cannot be structured or achievement evaluated. Audience education requires more than offering a few courses in music or art appreciation. It implies the opportunities to pursue programs for personal cultivation and satisfaction and the chance to develop new levels of sophistication as viewers

75

or listeners. Presumably courses in appreciation provide the knowledge, the grammar, and the familiarity with the art object to lead the student toward aesthetic judgments and discrimination. Only when opportunities are available to exercise critical judgment can the concern for the arts as an essential part of society be deepened.

Setting the conditions for audience education means recognizing where students are in their development and planning for the next higher step. It is a gross error to attempt the jump from the elementary to the most advanced in one step. It is better, sometimes, to commence with the familiar and unsophisticated or with the arts indigenous to a locale, then to weave in less familiar and more sophisticated art forms carefully and gradually.

The major weaknesses of this subtle kind of education result from programming based only on intuition and availability. There is agreement that programs in the arts seem good for people and that there is a steady increase in the amount, but precisely how effective the system is deserves some study. So far, the only answer is in terms of attendance or participation figures.

Colleges and universities appear intent on building sensitive, mature, and intelligent audiences and are having an increasingly greater effect on the status of the arts. This participation places them in a position to control both kind and quality. Possibly in time they may reverse the trend that currently oversupports pop artists.

What is the status of research and experimentation in the arts? As the arts have grown in importance on the campus, there has been new opportunity to review their purposes. Where once the primary goals of service and entertainment dominated, new goals call for innovation, leadership, and research. The university provides the culture in which new ideas, new talents, and new art forms

76

can flourish. Because the profit motive is not uppermost, risks and new directions can be permitted and failures withstood. (Unfortunately, even higher education abhors failure, so there is far less experimentation than one would surmise. Reportedly, only 3 per cent of university theater productions are original works, which means that the other 97 per cent are either standards, contemporary dramas, or Broadway musicals.) [14]

With more attention being paid to the development of artists and audience-building, the university is ideally suited to expose its students to new music, new theater, new art, and new dance. But financial support is not yet sufficient, except in rare instances, for total subsidization, so a compromise situation exists.

Supported research in the arts is in its infancy. Art historians, musicologists, and art educators have in their separate ways engaged in types of scholarly research. Much of it has been poorly supported, if at all, and much of it is carried out in the researcher's own time. With the newer possibilities offered by the National Endowment for the Arts, the U.S. Office of Education, and other sources of support, additional opportunities are opening. Nevertheless the scene is not bright, and international developments have clouded the picture somewhat. The approximately $7 million budgeted for support of the National Endowment for the Arts could easily be consumed just by the financially ailing symphonies. A portion of this money will find its way to the campus to encourage imaginative programs in education. (Ironically, however, the first money assigned to campuses made it possible for campus artists to escape in order to do their creative work elsewhere.)

One of the greatest needs for research and experimentation is in the area of methods of instruction as they relate to learning in the arts. This field has few examples

77

of serious study. Teaching problems are alleviated by larger lecture halls, more complicated slide projectors, and more teaching assistants. A few institutions are trying to work with television, but there is little documentation of their experiments and few attempts to evaluate their efforts. Louis Bright, associate commissioner of the Bureau of Research of the U.S. Office of Education, recently reported that the computer has great potential for teaching the fine arts—particularly music, drawing, and art—because, he explains, "it excels in teaching discrimination between what is good composition and what is not." [15] Many art educators would throw up their hands at the thought of programmed instruction, yet the very principles of programmed instruction are similar to the learning steps in art! In programmed instruction you proceed at your own rate, you learn in small steps in a somewhat orderly process, you receive immediate feedback and reinforcement, and you learn by an active process. This is not unlike the way some learning takes place in the arts. With the supply of competent teachers being rapidly absorbed, every conceivable means to assist instruction and to reduce educational waste needs to be explored, otherwise the arts will not be able to meet increased enrollments—another area that is not being adequately studied.

Some art educators are exploring computer-assisted instruction; others are studying teaching strategies, the relationships between educational theater and professional theater, problems of art learning, visual concept formation and visual training, curriculum construction, the use of instructional media, problems of motivation and evaluation, problems in aesthetic education, methods for the improvement of teaching and appreciation, methods in visual and auditory education, and a great variety of other problems. Unfortunately, many of these efforts, like the 1940

78

experiments of Hoyt Sherman at Ohio State,[16] frequently remain in isolation. Larger, massive efforts are needed immediately; what exists now are largely one-man efforts.

To summarize, the arts are firmly entrenched in higher education, and with the humanities are providing balance for science and technology. Students have demonstrated their hunger for the fine arts, and colleges and universities now attempt to satisfy that need through many approaches. The extent of the university's commitment and financial support to the performing arts places it in a unique role as a cultural leader. As such, it can now affect positively both quality and kinds of arts on a national level. It also has the opportunity for numerous shared activities and responsibilities with other organizations and institutions.

The diversity of students who are eager to engage in the arts as shown by their interests, levels of achievement, talents, and preparation calls for faculties of widely differing abilities and purposes. When students are grouped according to interests, abilities, or purposes they can be successfully guided and taught in the fine arts. They need, in addition to formal programs of instruction, opportunities for direct, personal confrontation with original works of art, live theater, music, and dance. Here they develop discrimination and critical judgment as well as indulge in personal enjoyment. A serious problem of education is how to help students remain open, receptive, and unbiased—able to be tolerant, even understanding, of the unusual experiments and thrusts of new theater, art, music, poetry, and dance while continuing to enjoy the traditional art forms.

Growing numbers of artists coming to campuses have stimulated even greater interest in the arts. In many cases, the artists are finding the university to be both supportive and enhancing. The academic community does know something about teaching the fine arts, and it is rapidly learning more. Some problems remain unanswered, but some may be unanswerable.

References

1. John A. Michaels, *Artists' Ideas About Art and Their Use in Education,* Final Report, Project #5-8300 (Washington, D.C.: U.S. Department of Health, Education and Welfare, Office of Education, Bureau of Research, 1967).
2. Jacob W. Getzels and Mihaly Czikszentmihaly, *Creative Thinking in Art Students,* Project #E-008 (Washington, D.C.: U.S. Department of Health, Education, and Welfare, Office of Education, Bureau of Research, 1964).
3. *The Performing Arts,* Rockefeller Panel Report on the Future of Theatre Dance, Music in America, Rockefeller Brothers Fund, Inc. (New York: McGraw-Hill, 1965), pp. 13–15.
4. "Sound and Fury in the Arts," *Look,* January 9, 1968, pp. 13–14.
5. *The Performing Arts, op. cit.,* p. 13.
6. National Arts and Humanities Foundations, *Hearings Before the Special Subcommittee on Arts and Humanities of the Committee on Labor and Public Welfare,* United States Senate, Eighty-Ninth Congress, February 25, 26; March 4, 5, 1965. Part II, pp. 404–407.
7. Gyorgy Kepes (Ed.), *Education of Vision* (New York: Braziller, 1965).
8. Edwin Bowell, "Campuses Drawing Cream of the Arts at Premium Prices," *New York Times,* January 15, 1968, p. 1.
9. *Ibid.*
10. W. McNeil Lowry, *The University and the Creative Arts,* Art Journal XX, *14*:233–239.

11. Michaels, *op. cit.,* pp. 112, 113.
12. Andrew C. Ritchie, *The Visual Arts in Higher Education,* College Art Association of America (New Haven, Conn.: Yale University Press, 1966).
13. *Music and Art in the Public Schools,* Research Monograph 1963-M3 (Washington, D.C.: National Education Association, Research Division, August 1963), p. 25.
14. Freda H. Goldman, *The Arts in Higher Adult Education* (Boston: Center for the Study of Liberal Education for Adults, Boston University, 1966), pp. 3, 4.
15. *Education U.S.A.: Washington Monitor* (Washington, D.C.: National School Public Relations Association, November 27, 1967), p. 78.
16. Hoyt L. Sherman, *Drawing by Seeing* (New York: Hinds, Hayden, and Eldredge, 1947).

V

Henry S. Dyer

College Testing and the Arts

Before considering the particular problem of college testing in the arts, I want to lay down a thesis about college testing in general. The thesis is that the combined effects of all the kinds of tests a college uses for all purposes whatever have more to do with the kind and quality of education the college offers than anything else the faculty may be doing, or thinks it is doing, to and for its students.

I first glimpsed the possibility of truth in this proposition about fifteen years ago when a certain liberal arts college invited me to look at the tests the instructors were using in their courses. The college had drawn up an extensive program in general education and was trying hard to do something significant about such now-familiar objectives as critical and creative thinking and sensitivity to the arts and human affairs. On paper it seemed like a good program, and there was considerable faculty involvement in making it succeed, but the dean and department heads were becoming troubled by increasing evidence that the program was not working as expected. There was excessive cutting of classes in the general education courses, accompanied by more successful last-minute cramming for examinations than seemed reasonable or normal. The amount of cheating was also disturbing. These kinds of student behavior seemed to the faculty somewhat less than consonant with the educational goals they had set for themselves and their students. What was wrong?

A review of the tests and examinations the professors were using in their courses suggested an obvious answer: practically none of the tests came reasonably close to testing the depths of knowledge, understanding, and sophisticated thinking implied by the high-minded objectives of the courses. The tests in all the subjects—the humanities, the arts, the sciences natural and social—*invited* cramming. They were overloaded with questions of the what-happened-where-when-how variety. They demanded scarcely anything more than straight memorization of lecture or textbook material. In a word, the academic reward system, insofar as it was embodied in the examinations, was seriously out of phase with the expectations of the instructors.

This episode suggested that the nature and quality of the tests instructors use to evaluate their students' course performance, and the comprehensive examinations frequently given to round off degree requirements, may be more determinative of the actual effects of instruction in any particular course, or program of courses, than the content and inspirational qualities of the instruction itself. What counts in the mind of the student are the kinds of operations the tests require him to perform, and these are

83

the operations that he will most likely learn to perform. If the tests and examinations used in courses are humdrum, as they so often are, then the student learning will be of the same humdrum variety. Hence the enormous importance of "good" tests—tests that really do measure the intellectual dimensions about which most college teachers profess to be concerned, and about which they hope their students will also be concerned.

In addition to keeping students informed on what is expected of them and how they are progressing in their course work, collegiate testing has two other principal functions that are less direct, but no less real, in their effects on how students learn. In most colleges these days testing plays a considerable if not a decisive part in the admissions process. Also, in many colleges testing is used in guidance to help students decide on their major field of study. Thus, to a considerable extent in some colleges and probably to some extent in all colleges, tests help to shape the character of the student body, both in the institution as a whole and in each of the major departments. Since it is generally conceded that the particular mix of talents and outlooks existing in a particular student body has a strong, possibly an overriding, influence on the way its members develop intellectually and otherwise, the tests used in admission and guidance, insofar as they help to determine the mix, play a role in shaping the academic environment that conditions the kind and amount of student learning that is likely to occur.

To these three functions of college testing—admissions, guidance, and the evaluation of course work—people professionally involved in testing usually add a fourth, namely, the feedback function. Effective testing, they say, *should* tell instructors and institutions where in particular they are succeeding and where they are failing to affect student learning, so that the instructional process can be kept effective at all times for all students. The feedback concept of testing is valid and laudable; it is one that in more hortatory moods I myself have urged. But it is an ideal that at the moment seems so far from realization in practice that its impact on the mental events that take place in classrooms or elsewhere on the campus is probably negligible.

The actual practice of testing in admissions, guidance, and the appraisal of end-of-course achievement, on the other hand, has a very powerful cumulative effect, for good or ill, on what colleges teach and students learn. The fact that most college faculties are probably unaware of the impact of the tests they use for these purposes makes the impact no less potent. Insofar as the testing is badly conceived or is misused or falls short of what it could be, by so much the quality of education supplied by the college is less than it might be. To put the matter in another way: effective testing in a college is as important a prerequisite to an effective educational program as is, for example, an adequate budget. If this sounds like propaganda for better testing, that of course is exactly what it is. I hope it is persuasive.

Given these premises, one arrives at the unhappy inference that education in the fine arts is seriously hobbled by the fact that testing in the arts is considerably less than adequate. A clue to the situation can be found in the amount of space allotted to reviews of tests in art and music in Buros' *Sixth Mental Measurements Yearbook*.[1] The Yearbook contains 1,365 pages of reviews of tests of all kinds. The percentage of this space allocated to each of six broad fields is approximately as follows:

85

Tests of academic achievement	38 per cent
Tests of character and personality	29 per cent
Tests of intelligence and aptitude	16 per cent
Vocational and sensory motor tests	11 per cent
Tests of nonacademic achievement	5 per cent
Tests of art and music	1 per cent

These figures give a crude but probably fairly accurate indication of the importance that test-makers—and, by implication, educators and the public that buys both tests and education—attach to both testing and education in the fine arts. By a wide margin, this kind of testing and education is clearly at the bottom of the heap. One is reminded of John Kenneth Galbraith's thesis that, in the new industrial state, aesthetic goals are given the lowest priority because they do not contribute to, and in fact are often in conflict with, the needs of the industrial system.

It would be comforting to suppose that the only action required to bring the arts into greater educational prominence would be to develop a larger number and wider variety of tests in the arts so as to make them more nearly competitive with the tests of conventional academic achievement and aptitude. Of course the causal sequence is not that simple. The paucity of testing in the arts is functionally related to the paucity of education in the arts. That is, the two conditions are, in a sense, mutually causative: if more and better tests in the fine arts were produced, probably more educators would see the wisdom of using them, and education in the fine arts would expand and improve. At the same time it seems unlikely that testers will give much more attention than they now do to the problems of testing in fine arts until a more serious demand for such tests arises in the colleges. It is perhaps of some significance in this connection that the

Advanced Test in Fine Arts was dropped from the Graduate Record Examination Program several years ago for want of an adequate market.

The tests in general use for college admission give no attention whatever to the arts. There are no such tests in either the American College Testing Program or the program of the College Entrance Examination Board. The main emphasis in both programs—and presumably this emphasis reflects the desires and aims of the colleges participating in them—is on mastery of the basic verbal and quantitative skills. The fact that tests of this kind of mastery tend to predict reasonably well the grades students get in most colleges suggests that, for the most part, *the whole system of secondary and higher education is a closed system from which the arts are, for all intents and purposes, excluded.* The situation was not really any different sixty years ago when the College Board was first getting under way: the tests then were vastly different in form and content, but not in the underlying verbal and quantitative abilities measured.

Attempts to break through this standard pattern of ability testing for admission to liberal arts colleges have been unsuccessful. I was involved in such an attempt in the early 1950's when the College Entrance Examination Board sought to bring into being for universal use a series of entrance examinations known as Tests of Developed Abilities. The goal was to create a series of tests to determine the mental processes believed to be important in each of three areas: science, social studies, and the humanities. The Test of Developed Abilities in the Humanities contained, among other things, two new, though still timid, departures from anything previously proposed for testing the typical candidate for the typical liberal arts college: namely, a test that required him to listen and re-

87

act to various passages of music and one that required him to look at and react to a series of pictures. In both cases the purpose was to see how much sensitivity to artistic forms the candidate might be bringing with him to college.

The Tests of Developed Abilities were stillborn. A committee of psychometric experts advised the College Board against their use on what has always seemed to me the irrelevant ground that the scores on the new tests were no more useful in predicting average college grades than were the verbal and quantitative scores of the Scholastic Aptitude Test, which was considerably shorter and cheaper. The pragmatic argument was decisive. No consideration was given to the possibility that by admitting some aesthetic dimensions into the entrance tests, one might have encouraged, if only in a small way, the exploration of new instructional dimensions in both school and college curricula.

The barrier to higher education in the arts is actually of course a succession of barriers beginning at least as far back as the secondary school, where serious attention to the arts is not ordinarily encouraged except perhaps as an extracurricular activity. Two investigators who have been concerned with the evaluation of student performance in secondary schools observe that:

> the junior high school is the point at which most students drop out of music and visual arts and only the talented continue. Hence there is no way to tell what the majority can or cannot do in these fields, or what factors in ability or perception differentiate those who will continue from those who will drop out [of art or music at the senior high school level].[2]

Even for the specially talented, however—those who do not "drop out" in junior high school—admission to a college where they hope to develop their special talents further may present some difficult, and possibly irrelevant, hurdles. See, for example, the admission requirements of the Philadelphia College of Art. According to the *College Handbook,* a "prime requirement for all applicants" to this college of art is that they shall submit for evaluation a portfolio containing a sampling of their best work in several modes. In addition, "students must rank in the top half of their class [unless] there is sufficient evidence of scholastic competence through tests, other records, and recommendations." [3] The test evidence of scholastic competence is that contained in the scores of the College Board's Scholastic Aptitude and Achievement Tests, which are "required of all candidates." Thus, even in a college that specializes in art, the admissions process appears to put considerable stress on purely academic ability as well as on artistic talent. Similarly, the Conservatory of Music at Oberlin College requires a performance audition for admission but also requires the College Board's Scholastic Aptitude and Achievement Tests of all candidates regardless of whether they are headed for the Conservatory or the liberal arts college.

A whole host of plausible reasons for the multiple test hurdles required of candidates in the performing and creative arts can be, and no doubt are, adduced by their proponents in the colleges concerned. One wonders whether the purely academic requirements for such specialists may not be unnecessarily high and therefore self-defeating. Be this as it may, however, it is clear that in the case of liberal arts colleges the general effect of admission requirements is to exclude aesthetically gifted students who may have trouble with the kind of abstract reasoning and manipulation of words and symbols demanded by the usual academic tests of aptitude and achievement. Much

89

too little is known about the effects of this kind of exclusion on college subcultures and on programs in secondary education that are still dominated, probably more than secondary educators themselves realize or are prepared to admit, by the admission requirements of the "better" colleges.

Part of the reason that aptitude tests in the arts are little used in the college admissions process is that the tests available have failed to inspire confidence. The lack of confidence is justified. As suggested by the figures given above from the *Sixth Mental Measurements Yearbook,* the amount of psychometric expertise being invested in tests of art and music is remarkably small compared to the amount going into other kinds of psychological tests. This condition has prevailed for a long time, with the result that aptitude tests in art are considerably inferior to aptitude tests in other fields. Anne Anastasi, in her standard work on psychological testing, explains why:

> The development of tests specifically designed for measuring aesthetic abilities . . . has been slow and sporadic. Little progress in the testing of artistic, musical, or literary aptitudes has been made since the early 1940's. In number, scope, and technical refinements, tests in this area have lagged far behind other aptitude tests.[4]

Anastasi finds two reasons for the lag: the suspicion in which all quantitative measurement of artistic products and talents is held by artists and teachers of art; and (anticipating Galbraith) the "value system of the contemporary culture" in which "the demand for testing office clerks, engineers, and Air Force pilots has proved more widespread and more insistent than the demand for testing poets, musicians, or painters."[5]

The principal contribution that well-seasoned specialized aptitude tests can make in the college setting is of two kinds. They can help identify, from among a mass of students, those who will have the best chance of succeeding in a particular field of study, and they can contribute to the individual student's decision process by helping him get a better idea of his own possibilities in each of several fields. Having made this statement, let me hasten to underline the fact that *no* aptitude test can make a full contribution to these processes; that is, *no* aptitude test, or combination of aptitude tests, can provide definitive and infallible information on how a student *will* make out in one field as compared with another.

One might suppose at this late date that such a caution would no longer be necessary. One might suppose that educators and educated people generally would long since have dispensed with the ancient myth of the heritability of specific talents, and would finally have realized that the most any and all aptitude tests can do is to provide uncertain extrapolations of the quality of an individual's future learning based on a somewhat less than adequate sample of what he has learned in the past. Suppositions of this sort may seem eminently reasonable to anyone who has worked long enough with aptitude tests to feel the full weight of their problems and limitations; but in fact the precepts of psychological measurement and the mountains of ignorance about the nature and development of human talent that still remain untouched by the behavioral sciences are still ordinarily unknown to the majority of thinking people. Teatime conversations about testing and the development of talents are still couched in metaphoric terms that reflect an unawareness of the kinds of constructs that are permissible on the basis of present knowledge. Expressions like "the nurture of natural endowments," "the search for hidden talents," or "making the most of one's gifts" are in this category, and they encourage the mistaken and misleading analogy that aptitude tests are more or less like mental Geiger counters capable of "detecting" something that is already "there" inside the individual.

The most any well-seasoned specialized aptitude tests can do for a college admissions office, a college counseling office, or a student who is wondering about his educational and career plans is to contribute a little something to an assessment of the relative probabilities of the student's future performance in each of a number of fields. What I am calling "well-seasoned specialized aptitude tests" are those that have been widely used in a great many institutions with a great many students—tests on which enough follow-up data have accumulated so that the degree to which the test scores do contribute to the clarification of the relative probabilities is known, at least to some useful approximation.

Aptitude tests in music and art—even those that have been around for a long time—are not in this sense "well-seasoned." There have been literally thousands of studies to try to determine how helpful tests of verbal and quantitative aptitude are in the prediction of grades in various kinds of colleges, whereas similar studies involving tests of artistic aptitude can be reckoned only in the dozens. We know, for instance, that the scores on the mathematical section of the College Board's Scholastic Aptitude Test reduces the amount of error in the prediction of grades at engineering schools by a factor, on the average, of about 15 per cent. We have little similar information on such well-known aptitude tests in the visual arts as the Meier Art Tests,[6] or the more recent Horn Art Aptitude Inventory.[7] A few studies on these tests, some running back into the 1930's, have indicated positive correlations be-

92

tween their scores and student's grades in art courses or ratings on the quality of creative work. More recently, studies involving the Architectural Aptitude Test [8] have shown similar correlations with grades in colleges of architecture. Even so, there is still a tremendous amount to be learned about the specific qualities of performance that are most likely to characterize candidates who will subsequently succeed and contribute in a major and creative way to these fields.

The aptitude tests in music are in a similar plight. Anastasi's comment on the oldest and best known, the Seashore Tests of Musical Talent,[9] summarizes the general state of affairs.

> It is undoubtedly true that ability to discriminate pitch, loudness, timbre, and other properties of tones is essential to both appreciation and production of music. To predict musical achievement, however, we need to know much more. What is the minimum cutoff point for different kinds of musical activities? Is there any correlation between test scores and musical performance beyond the cutoff point? What is the relative importance of each of the functions measured by the tests, both in relation to each other and in relation to the entire array of requisite traits? [10]

The Wing Standardized Tests of Musical Intelligence are a recent English development that goes beyond the atomistic approach to measurement of musical aptitude that has always characterized the Seashore Tests and that has long been regarded by many professionally concerned persons as a serious limitation. The Wing Tests employ recognizable musical content, include more complex kinds of analysis than the Seashore Tests, and get at certain aspects of aesthetic appreciation. They look promising, but data on how well their promise is being realized in the actual prediction of various kinds of musical achievement are still few.

It seems unlikely that there will be much progress in the development of aptitude tests in any of the arts until the available tests, even in their present dubious state, are actually used in vastly greater numbers and the predictive powers of their scores investigated for many kinds of students undergoing many kinds of learning experiences in many different colleges. It is the nature of aptitude tests in any field that only as they are used in a variety of situations can they improve.

Even so, the upper limit of improvement of any aptitude test is determined by the quality of the measures of later achievement that it is supposed to predict. In the case of aptitude tests in the arts this limitation is severe, for measures of college achievement in the arts have been unsatisfactory. The fundamental reason is that the dimensions of this kind of achievement are still largely undefined in the minds of professors. The typical measure of artistic achievement has consisted of course grades based on unspecified evidences of student performance as judged by instructors, each of whom has his own privately determined and usually unarticulated criteria for differentiating work that is in good taste from work that is in poor taste, or work that is excellent from work that is shoddy, or work that is creative from work that is dull and unimaginative. The confusion is often further compounded by failure to distinguish explicitly among the four principal variables that can be involved in an approach to the arts: creative production, performance, analysis, and affective response. Similar difficulties exist in other areas of educational achievement, but they are especially acute in the arts because of the inherent lack of objective standards and the consequent disagreements among the professors and practitioners about what actually constitutes excellence in the arts.

It is partly for this reason, no doubt, that so many of the courses in the humanities offered by most liberal arts colleges avoid the issue altogether by concentrating on *knowledge about* the arts rather than *performance in* the arts. Instructors seem to have an underlying fear that to *grade* the typical student amateur [11] on his ability in such activities as painting, singing, composing music, dancing, acting, playwriting, or on his affective responses to such productions and performances (that is, his "appreciation") runs the risk not only of being unfair because of the biases growing out of the instructor's own predilections, but also of killing off any tender enthusiasms for the arts that might be starting to sprout. The fear is well founded, since performance in and response to the arts can scarcely conform to the arbitrary one-dimensional standards, which is what grades essentially are, without losing their primary significance as human experience. Grading by its very nature is a threat to the student and can drive him away from the fine arts altogether.

How is the dilemma to be met? David Riesman has made an intriguing and, I think, wise suggestion on the score. He says:

> . . . it seems important to try to distinguish analytically between the intertwined functions of grading and testing, for it is testing which students often seek in order to determine their own capacities, while grading ranks these capacities in some necessarily arbitrary way in terms of relative invidiousness and prestige. . . . Testing [is] an inescapable part of the educational, indeed of the larger developmental process: young people want to measure themselves against the environment

95

(including their fellows) in various ways, and testing also at its best contributes to the security of their inner standards and their confidence in their ability to perform. Someone who has never been tested may harbor delusions of grandeur or misery; he is not likely to develop autonomous yet valid standards that transcend yet take account of those of his environment.[12]

If one follows Riesman's logic into the creative and performing arts, the idea becomes compelling that what we must try to find is some system for *testing without grading.* There is a good deal to be said for such a solution, even though it may contain more subtleties than ordinarily meet the academic eye.

How is it possible to test a student and provide him with meaningful information about the quality of his artistic performance without *in effect* grading him, that is, ranking his performance "in some necessarily arbitrary way"? The answer, I think, lies in a method of assessment that *exploits,* rather than bypasses, the inevitable disagreements that occur among experts and others about what constitutes excellent performance in any of the arts. This approach is in sharp contrast to the usual one of trying to force judgments of students' artistic productions into what is essentially a meaningless consensus by averaging or suppressing differences of opinion (as, for instance, in the case of the "jury" that rates a student's performance of a sonata, or the work a student painter presents for the master's degree). It is an approach that recognizes that there can be, and usually are, a number of "schools of thought" concerning those qualities in a student's work—or in any artistic production—by which the work is to be judged good or poor. That is, it delineates differences in aesthetic values but imposes none, and thereby leaves the student free to select the system of values by which, if he chooses, he may assess his own performance. The assumption, according to Riesman, is that he *will* so choose, that most students will feel the need of some set of externally determined values at the outset against which to test themselves, and that only so will they eventually arrive at a self-determined set of values that is valid for them. Implicit in this view of the matter is the broader view that in a liberal education the prime function of the arts—and of the humanities generally—is to provide students with a chance to work out their own values in such a disciplined manner that they will feel comfortable with their own heresies. In a time largely characterized by mindless conformity, it seems to me this educational goal is of the first order of importance as one having to do with both the means as well as the reasons for human survival.

In this scheme of educational priorities, then, the great task prerequisite to any effective college testing in the fine arts is that of delineating as concretely as possible the current "schools of thought" in any particular field and translating them into some test or other device whereby the student can apply any evaluative criteria he may choose to his own work or to that of others. The task of delineation, of identifying the current dimensions of judgment in any of the arts, is an enormous one that has only just begun to engage the attention of a handful of psychometricians. Such studies as there are, however, may help to illustrate and define the problem.

One of the earliest studies had to do with student writing. It was conducted by Paul B. Diederich, Sydell T. Carlton, and John W. French in the 1950's, and has been reported by French under the title "Schools of Thought in Judging Excellence of English Themes." [13] To use French's terminology, the purpose of the experiment was to explore "reader disagreement, or in more elegant terms, the dimensionality in the grading behavior of the readers [of student themes]." That is, it sought to discover the extent to which a mixed group of concerned adults may differ in the qualities they judge to be most important in good writing. A further question asked of the study was whether the clustering of judges with respect to the kinds of writing performance they tend to prize appears to have any relation to the professions in which they are engaged. Accordingly, a group of English teachers, social scientists, natural scientists, writers, editors, lawyers, and business executives read and rated 300 student essays, each according to his own unaided judgment of what differentiates superior writing from inferior writing. The statistical operation of inverse factor analysis was performed on the ratings thus obtained. This is a technique for identifying the clusters of judges within which agreement tends to be high. It puts no constraints on the system, however, with respect to either the number of clusters or the number of judges in any cluster: if there are no identifiable "schools of thought" among the judges, for example, that fact can emerge from the data.

In point of fact, five clusters of judges emerged. An exhaustive analysis was then made of comments made by representatives from each cluster—comments on *why* they rated each theme as they did. It appeared that one group of judges rated the papers primarily on the *ideas* they contained; a second group was chiefly concerned with the *form* of the writing; a third group with its *flavor;* a fourth group with *mechanics;* and a fifth with *wording.* These five rubrics—ideas, form, flavor, mechanics, and wording—are not altogether satisfactory for describing the features of the writing that each group emphasized; they are merely a kind of rough shorthand to suggest in a general way how the five schools of thought differ. One of the interesting incidental findings of the study was that the clustering of the readers around the qualities they preferred seemed to bear practically no relationship to the professions they followed. For instance, some social scientists, some natural scientists, some writers, some businessmen, and some lawyers are prominently identified with the cluster emphasizing ideas, while others in these same fields are to be found elsewhere.

There is, of course, nothing definitive about this study of schools of thought in judging student writing. If the study were to be replicated on a different mix of readers with a different set of themes, or better still, poems—and as far as I know it has not been—the number and nature of the clusters of judges to emerge might appear quite different. The main point of the study for the present purpose is that it illustrates the tremendous complexity of the problem of actually identifying and empirically characterizing the schools of thought that form around the act of judging performance in writing. It also suggests that there is much work to be done before the judgmental dimensions—these multiple and largely incongruent criteria of good writing—can be incorporated into tests of writing.

A second series of studies has similarly investigated judgments of student drawings. In this case the drawings were produced by 191 sophomores in the Rhode Island School of Design. The judges consisted of seven instructors from the Rhode Island School of Design itself, seven from Cooper Union, ten from Pratt Institute, and four non-artists. The analysis in this particular study turned up three principal clusters of judges (that is, schools of thought). Unlike the clustering found in the judgments of student writing, the three groups of judges tended to be strongly, though not exclusively, identified with their professional origins. One cluster consisted of the instructors from the Rhode Island School of Design itself, a second cluster consisted mostly of those from Cooper Union and Pratt Institute, and the third cluster consisted of the four non-artists plus one instructor from Pratt Institute.

The outcomes of this analysis are not unexpected. That the instructors in the Rhode Island School of Design clearly form a single and fairly cohesive school of aesthetic thought is no doubt partly a result of their working together, partly a result of the fact that they were judging the work of their own students, and partly a result of the fact that they chose that particular institution in which to teach, or were chosen by it. The "outside artists" (the group from Cooper Union and Pratt) apparently tended to form a different school of thought mainly because they were subject to a different set of common influences than were operating for the first group. And the non-artists made up a cluster by themselves simply because they were, in fact, laymen having laymen's tastes that, not surprisingly, differ in fairly radical ways from the tastes of practicing artists.

Klein, in the final study of the series,[14] finds that the criteria for judging the drawings differ in important ways among the three clusters. The instructors in the Rhode Island School of Design tended to give high ratings to drawings that give an effect of "spontaneousness" as contrasted with "deliberateness." The judgments of the group of experts from the other two institutions were uniquely characterized by a preference for drawings that minimized realism and that depended on the use of shading and shapes as a principle of organization. The judgments of the non-artist group rated high the pictures that were strong on neatness and photographic realism and

100

rated low those that tended to give an impression of chaos and disorder.

A study at the Chicago Art Institute by Getzels and Czikszentmihaly,[15] though employing a methodological approach different from the Rhode Island studies, nevertheless bears out the finding that, relative to other groups of judges, the instructors in an art institute tend to agree in their opinions of what constitutes excellent performance by the students who have been through the institute. Otherwise, the Chicago study suggests that any generalizations one might be tempted to make on the sole basis of the Rhode Island study may be very tenuous indeed. The Chicago study used drawings produced by senior students at the Art Institute of Chicago. These drawings were rated by groups of judges: instructors at the Institute, other practicing artists, and graduate students in mathematics and business at the University of Chicago. The most homogeneous group of judgments came from the instructors, the least homogeneous from the practicing artists. At least one finding in the Chicago study that would hardly have been predicted from the Rhode Island study is that the non-artists (the mathematics and business students) tended to agree strongly with both the practicing artists and the art teachers in their preference for "abstract" as against "realistic" drawings. This outcome could be peculiar to Chicago since the two "non-artist" groups were composed of generally sophisticated individuals whose opinions had been no doubt affected by the atmosphere of the university in which they were students.

These studies are only the barest first attempts to come to some understanding of the multiple and often conflicting criteria that must be defined in all the arts before the development of meaningful tests of artistic per-

101

formance can even begin. The few pioneer studies have barely scratched the surface of only two areas of student performance—writing and drawing. As far as I have been able to discover, *no* similar efforts have been made anywhere to explore the schools of thought in any of the other creative or performing arts—music, dance, the theater arts, and so on. We do indeed have much to learn about college testing in the arts before it will be able to serve any other than the routine and essentially noneducational function of grading students on the facts they have memorized about art and artists.

In this chapter I have focused on college testing in the arts as a strong determiner of the amount and quality of college education in the arts. I have suggested that unless and until such testing is vastly improved and is disentangled from the dubious practice of grading students in these fields, the kinds of learning in the arts that the typical college student acquires will be small and largely unrelated to the direct aesthetic experiences that are, or ought to be, involved in producing, performing, analyzing, and responding to works of art. Finally, I have tried to make the point that the needed improvements in testing in the arts, and by implication the needed improvements in liberal education in the arts, are unlikely to materialize until we come to terms with the fact that the world of art is a world of multiple standards that are in need of far clearer empirical delineation than they have had up to now.

One of the truths we know, but find deeply troublesome in both teaching and testing, is that in art there is never only one "right" answer to such questions as, What is good? What is effective? What is excellent? There are instead many possible "right" answers. The task of liberal education in the arts is to stimulate and help the individual student to search for those answers that are "right" for him. In the course of his search he needs some means of testing out his own aesthetic values against those of others in order to get an increasingly clear sense of where he is and where he is going. To provide him with this kind of testing will require on the part of both testers and teachers a fundamentally new conceptualization of the nature and functions of college testing in the arts. This new way of looking at these matters will take a considerable amount of time and effort to achieve because it must be accompanied by a similarly new conceptualization of the nature and functions of college testing in the arts. I have to believe that both sorts of reorientation are possible, for otherwise the world my grandchildren are going to inherit, if any, looks to be more bleak than one likes to contemplate.

References

1. Oscar K. Buros, *The Sixth Mental Measurements Yearbook* (Highland Park, N.J.: The Gryphon Press, 1965).
2. Frances R. Link and Paul B. Diederich, "A Cooperative Evaluation Program," in *Evaluation as Feedback and Guide* (Washington, D.C.: Association for Supervision and Curriculum Development, 1967), p. 165.
3. College Entrance Examination Board, *The College Handbook, 1967–69* (New York: College Entrance Examination Board, 1967).
4. Anne Anastasi, *Psychological Testing* (New York: Macmillan, 1961). This quotation is from the 1961 edition, but Anastasi informs me that the forthcoming edition will record little further progress in the testing of aptitudes in art and music.
5. *Ibid.*
6. Norman C. Meier, *The Meier Art Tests* (Iowa City: Uni-

103

versity of Iowa, Bureau of Research and Service, 1929–1963).

7. C. C. Horn, *Horn Art Aptitude Inventory* (Chicago: Stoelting, 1951–1953).

8. Educational Testing Service, *Architectural School Aptitude Test: Bulletin of Information for Candidates, 1967–68* (Princeton, N.J.: Educational Testing Service, 1967).

9. Carl E. Seashore and others, *Seashore Measures of Musical Talents* (New York: Psychological Corporation, 1919–1960).

10. Anastasi, *op. cit.*

11. I use the noun *amateur* in its original meaning as one who engages in an activity for the sheer love of it; it is not to be equated here with dilettantism.

12. David Riesman, "The Impact of Examinations," in *Examining in Harvard College* (Cambridge: Faculty of Arts and Sciences, Harvard University, 1963), pp. 71–87.

13. John W. French, "Schools of Thought in Judging Excellence of English Themes," in Anne Anastasi (Ed.), *Testing Problems in Perspective* (Washington, D.C.: American Council on Education, 1966), pp. 587–596.

14. Stephen P. Klein, *A Description of Points of View in Esthetic Judgments in Terms of Similarity Dimensions,* Research Bulletin 67-53 (Princeton, N.J.: Educational Testing Service, 1967).

15. Jacob W. Getzels and M. Czikszentmihaly, "Aesthetic Opinion: An Empirical Study," *Public Opinion Quarterly* (in press).

VI

Lewis B. Mayhew

The Arts and Access to Higher Education

The fine and performing arts (music, painting, sculpture, drama, dance, and the minor arts) currently seem ascendant in American society. And since institutions of higher education are such important parts of that society, the arts are presumed to be ascendant there also. But such an assumption rests on conflicting evidence and opinion.

The national potential significance of the arts is well revealed in the Rockefeller Brothers Panel Report on the *Future of Theatre, Dance, Music in America:*

> Many social and political forces have combined at this moment of history, both to compel interest in the arts and to justify that interest in practical terms. The intersection of these forces provides an unparalleled opportunity for the arts and the na-

105

tion, particularly since it occurs at a moment when a surge of vitality in the arts themselves has brought their needs and their delights to the attention of the national consciousness, as never before. . . . The panel is motivated by the conviction that the arts are not for a privileged few but for the many, that their place is not on the periphery of society but at its center, that they are not just a form of recreation but are of central importance to our well being and happiness. In the panel's view, this status will not be widely achieved unless artistic excellence is the constant goal of every artist and every arts organization, and mediocrity is recognized as the ever present enemy of true progress in the development of the arts.[1]

Such a belief was made an essential part of national policy when on September 29, 1965, President Johnson signed into law authorization for the establishment of a National Foundation on the Arts and the Humanities. This foundation is empowered to make matching grants to groups and organizations for work of substantial artistic and cultural significance. It may commission works, develop workshops to improve public appreciation of the arts, engage in planning to encourage public enjoyment of the arts, and even provide facilities in which artists can work. In short, national awareness of the significance of the arts is thus envisioned as growing to equal that currently concerning the sciences.

Whether such a policy stance will result in genuine artistic advance within the culture is at present seriously debated. Elitists such as Dwight MacDonald believe that the only result of such a national concern for the arts must be the triumph of masscult, which, he believes, does not have even the theoretical possibility of being good. Masscult, which must result from mass effort, is not just unsuccessful art. "It is non-art. It isn't even anti-art." [2] On the other hand, democratic optimists contend that both bases for support and appreciation of the arts can be widened; they argue that the qualitative level of art presented to the public is rising, and that as long as the people have a major voice in policy the rise can continue.

In a sense the outcome of such a debate might well be decided by what role the nation's colleges and universities play in the relatively near future. In James Perkins' mind, "The university has become one of the great institutions of the modern world. In the United States it is central in the conduct of our national life. It is the most sophisticated agency we have for advancing knowledge through scholarship and research. It is crucial in the transmittal of knowledge from one generation to the next." [3]

If this is so, there is considerable room to question how the arts will fare. In one student's opinion, the arts have moved in on higher education with enough impact to bring about a basic change in the ecology of culture in America. Not only are the channels of distribution of culture changed, but the arts have radically modified both the curriculum and the climate of campus life. Today colleges offer appreciation and applied courses in the arts, encourage extracurricular amateur art activity, erect expensive new arts facilities, and serve as the most rapidly growing impresario for the bulk of the nation's artists.[4]

Although he would agree with the intention of such an optimistic statement, Harold Taylor finds that such an ideal is far from being realized.

> Yet so recent is the concern of the society for the arts as an element in the popular culture and so recent and sudden is the expansion of the potential and actual audience for the arts, that the educational system is not ready either for the artists or

107

their audiences. On the contrary, the educational system has done its best to keep the arts and their practitioners outside and to eliminate systematically from admission all those whose talents lie in the arts, in favor of students who were adept in the scholastic exercises. In the elementary schools only 10 per cent of all teaching in the visual arts is done by persons who have had any experience in the field.[5]

Taylor's concern leads straight to the dilemma the nation's colleges and universities face. American higher education has long performed the three functions of teaching, research, and service, but it has typically considered that much of its teaching was to prepare people for vocations and callings. Whether it was a colonial college that prepared ministers and political leaders, a land-grant college that prepared scientific farmers, or a modern university that prepared medical doctors and future research workers, the institution's primary mission was a professional or vcoational one. And until as recently as the end of World War II the bulk of the research done was intended to feed into that teaching function. Similarly, services were seen as direct outgrowths of the two other functions, as in the case of extension programs, which were considered offshoots from the on-campus teaching program. Further, the nature of vocations and callings has generally been circumscribed by the limits of what was deemed appropriate college-level work and by the austere Calvinism that has so influenced the American character. General or liberal education has in practice been considered either the best vocational training for certain callings or a needed canvas on which the real work regarding one's profession can be viewed in perspective.

Except for some work in music and dramatics and

108

except at a few colleges such as Bennington, Sarah Lawrence, and Stephens, extensive work in the fine arts has not been offered until quite recently. Studio courses in painting, ballet, and the minor arts were somehow regarded as more appropriate for the extracurriculum, from which point they would not interfere with the more serious curricular activities. But times have changed. Whether the premise is that of Edward Gordon—that the most crucial task facing the college is to prepare people for a lifetime of leisure—or that of Thomas H. Hamilton—that the arts comprise a major way of looking at reality—or the idea that the colleges are the last remaining hope for training artists and displaying the results of their work, the belief seems to grow that the arts should figure strongly in the life of each college and university.

If this is to happen, ways must be prepared for artists to feel comfortable in a university setting (this means setting aside traditional reward systems), and channels must be opened for students with interests or talents in the arts to enter the university without feeling unduly guilty and without jeopardizing their primary interests. Clearly, neither of these two conditions at present prevails. Before they can, and before steps can be taken to ensure that they will, it is necessary to examine the current situation.

The evidence regarding such matters is fugitive and somewhat inconclusive, but at least the outline of the present situation can be inferred. First, it is becoming increasingly clear that the normal predictors of academic success and the devices used to screen students in or out of college bear little or no relationship to either performance or creativity in the arts. "Among artists such as painters, sculptors, and designers, the correlation between rated quality of work and measured intelligence is zero or slightly negative. . . . Over the total range of intelligence and creativity a low positive correlation, probably in the neighborhood of .40, obtains; beyond an IQ of about 120, however, measured intelligence is a negligible factor in creativity, and the motivational and stylistic variables upon which our own research has laid such stress are the major determiners in creativity." [6] Achievement in college in such things as artistic, musical, speech, and dramatic activities has little relationship to either measured academic potential or to academic success. For nonacademic achievement the best predictor of accomplishment in college is similar accomplishment in high school. This point is well made in the following tables.

TABLE 1

RELATIONSHIP OF ACT TESTS AND HIGH SCHOOL GRADES TO
COLLEGE ACHIEVEMENT FOR MALE COLLEGE SOPHOMORES *

Achievement	ACT English	ACT Mathematics	ACT Social Studies	ACT Natural Science	High School Grade Point Average
Speech and Drama	06	—05	03	—07	—01
Artistic	05	—06	04	—01	—01
Musical	03	—06	—02	02	00

* Richards, Jr., James M., and others. *The Prediction of Student Accomplishment in College.* Iowa City: American College Testing Program, June 1966. Research Report No. 13.

TABLE 2

RELATIONSHIP BETWEEN HIGH SCHOOL AND COLLEGE ACTIVITIES *

	Speech and Drama	Art	Music
Drama	44	—02	15
Art	12	49	10
Music	16	01	35

* Richards, Jr., James M., and others. *The Prediction of Student Accomplishment in College.* Iowa City: American College Testing Program, June 1966. Research Report No. 13.

110

Since admission to college in selective institutions and guidance and placement in even nonselective institutions is usually based on high school rank in class and performance on one of the several academic aptitude or achievement tests, these judgments are made for the most part without regard for such things as the performing arts. "It is possible that those who achieve in art rate highly on certain types of intelligence measures but not on standard tests of intelligence which depend on verbal, computational and related abilities in which they are apt to be deficient."[7] And a similar, though less pronounced, tendency is found with respect to musical talent.

Not only in selecting students for college, but in collegiate programs themselves, does lack of concern for the performing arts and their requisite skills manifest itself. In recent years one of the more popular collegiate innovations has been honors programs. One of the earlier attempts was that at Swarthmore, which began in 1922. But especially since Sputnik, colleges have been afraid that they were not providing for the most gifted and talented of their students. Generally, these programs have emphasized the student's intellectual, analytical, critical, and research powers, not his creative, intuitive, or symbolic powers.[8] Honors programs usually identify students early, continue through four years, make work flexible but with due provision for fields of concentration, seek to be visible, use techniques of independent work suitable for honors students, provide a faculty of considerable intellectual power, and arrange for students to interact often with the faculty. Students who do honors work clearly reflect this intellective analytical style. They had good high school records and high scores on aptitude tests, and recognized the need to enter college. They had been active in extracurricular activities in high school, held elective posi-

111

tions in student government, participated in athletics, and had been featured in dramatic presentations and in orchestras. During their freshman year these honors students devoted long hours to books and assignments through fear of competition and faculty or parental disapproval, but showed little delight in their learning. Still they found time to engage in some out-of-class work in college, which typically involved the student newspaper, athletics, and musical or dramatic activities.[9]

Now clearly there are colleges that value the arts, use interest or competence in them as one dimension for screening students, and consider curricular participation in the arts as worthy as courses in chemistry, history, or mathematics. Bennington, Sarah Lawrence, and Stephens are among those. But generally, in the present climate, academic excellence is confined to the more orthodox academic subjects. This point is well made by a Columbia professor discussing a revision of the humanities course. "I hate sensibility. I hate perceptivity. All I care about is the mind." [10]

Generally, students from a variety of fields or subjects, if they are expected to gain some understanding of the creative life of man, will do so in either a general education course in the humanities or a departmental course used to satisfy a humanities requirement. But rarely are these courses explicitly concerned with the fine arts. Fisher, examining humanities courses in many different institutions, finds that the most common type of course is one that adopts a historical cultural approach.[11] More than three-fourths of the institutions have humanities courses that use a chronological framework. They may offer a history of civilization course, a cultural epoch plan, a religiously oriented course, or an intensive treatment of a few highly creative periods. Out of these has come the next

112

most popular approach, the philosophical course in which great issues, frequently as reflected in great books, are discussed. Although colleges have recently tried to instill some elements of the fine arts into the humanities effort through such devices as lending records and prints through the library, the emphasis on the creative arts is clearly a minority one. An even smaller number of courses try to give students some direct studio experience; for example, the University of Chicago has maintained a workshop studio, but participation is voluntary.[12]

Bell, in his recommendations for a revision of the general education program of Columbia College, illustrates both an interesting minority belief and an enormous naïveté about secondary schools when he remarks, "The music and fine arts humanities courses, even more than the first-year course, are organized on the premise that a student is best initiated in aesthetic experience by confronting him with masterpieces from our cultural heritage. I have suggested that because students in the secondary schools are now so greatly exposed to culture both in school and through the mass media, these humanities courses should be examined with a view to devoting more attention to the nature of visual forms in the arts and new forms of sound in music." He proposed further that since some freshmen can be expected to show proficiency in music or art, those who could be exempted from, say, the music course be allowed to devote a year to the visual arts, and a student exempted from fine arts to spend a year in music.[13] In a survey of the state of humanities requirements in 289 Southern regional institutions, it was found that 243 (84 per cent) required English, 196 (67.8 per cent) history, 114 (39.4 per cent) literature, 57 (19.7 per cent) art, 64 (22.1 per cent) religion, 38 (13.1 per cent) music, and 18 (6.2 per cent) philosophy.[14]

113

In explaining opinions of college faculty and administration about the role of art and music courses, Anderson said, "Art requirements, where there are such, are not, it seems, generally resented or criticized. But where they are lacking, sentiment is only slightly more in favor of something being done about it than not. With music it is about the same thing. Deans and humanities people occasionally express a kind of nostalgic longing for something more in those areas for students, but, in the same breath, a kind of resignation as well that there is probably little or nothing that can be done. Generally they seem to feel that the best possible arrangement is a multiple-choice one, admitting at the same time that where a broad choice is permitted, the previous conditioning of students generally makes for a four- or five-to-one choice for something other than art courses. Many point to the pressure of departmental interests, particularly those of a more 'practical' sort—sociology, psychology and the like—and the consequent difficulty of having such things as art and music even considered as essentials. At only a few are other means of providing significant experience in these areas for students being sought. Two, for example, are now projecting four-year assembly series planned to acquaint their students in a systematic and effective way with these areas.

"Many art and music teachers do not want requirements in these areas. Some hold the conviction that these fields are for an elect. Others shudder at having to offer required courses with their usual burden of unselected students. There are many, too, who still feel that instruction, to be really effective, must be individualized, a position from which professors of literature and history seem to have been generally routed. Only rarely was there a man in art or music who seemed genuinely concerned that every student on the campus have some significant experience with his specialty." [15] This preciousness about the fields of the arts is probably responsible for the separateness between art and music departments that we see on so many liberal arts college campuses. It is also involved in the fact that science departments typically allow undergraduate majors to take work in the arts, but arts and humanities departments are not so inclined. They keep their majors well within the fold.[16]

Clearly art and music are considered an extra and an ornament to the education of college students, while other generally accepted liberal arts and sciences are judged to be, if not essential, at least of greater worth.

Most professional faculty members believe that all students should study English composition, but see how they compare economics (frequently not even taught as general education) with art and music, as shown in Table 3.

TABLE 3

ATTITUDES OF PROFESSIONAL FACULTY MEMBERS
TOWARD CERTAIN LIBERAL ARTS COURSES *

	Economics		Art		Music	
	Re-quired of All	Dis-couraged or Pro-hibited	Re-quired by All	Dis-couraged or Pro-hibited	Re-quired by All	Dis-couraged or Pro-hibited
Total	45.1	2.5	12.1	7.1	13.0	6.4
Agriculture	57.1	.6	4.7	10.3	2.1	11.8
Business	85.2	—	6.9	6.9	4.7	11.1
Education	28.9	1.2	25.3	1.5	22.3	7.2
Engineering	56.1	1.6	2.7	13.3	1.7	13.8
Home Economics	77.8	—	44.4	—	16.7	—
Journalism	63.5	1.5	14.4	4.0	4.5	9.0
Music	4.8	14.5	29.1	1.4	64.4	.6
Nursing	15.1	1.6	10.4	4.1	5.0	3.8
Pharmacy	62.1	—	3.1	13.6	1.1	17.9

* Dressel, Paul L., Lewis B. Mayhew, and Earl J. McGrath. *The Liberal Arts as Viewed by Faculty Members in Professional Schools.* New York: Teachers College, Columbia University, 1959.

115

The same climate, hostile toward or at least unconcerned about the fine arts, is reflected in several major testing ventures. Whether the testing government follows or leads educational practice is immaterial in this regard. Both educational practice and large-scale testing reflect a similar bias. The Educational Testing Service offers a number of programs. The National Guidance Testing Program offers ability and achievement tests in reading, writing, listening, mathematics, science, and social studies. The Secondary School Admission Tests assess scholastic ability and reading comprehension. The Preliminary Scholastic Aptitude Test concentrates only on verbal and mathematical reasoning, as does the Scholastic Aptitude Test. But the SAT Achievement Tests do not include tests in art, music, drama, or the other fine arts, nor does the Advanced Placement Program. (Examinations are available in American history, biology, chemistry, English, European history, French, German, Latin, mathematics, physics, and Spanish.) The Graduate Record Examination Program does offer the humanities as one of the area tests, and the Teacher Education Program does offer one-sixteenth of the basic tests in the fine arts. Industrial arts—and this is scarcely art in the sense implied here—and music education are the only art- and music-related subjects available for the teaching field tests.[17]

Even instruments intended to assess a college's intellectual climate environment reflect the feeling that the fine arts are really not very important. The College and University Environment Scale consists of 150 statements; students are supposed to indicate whether or not each statement applies to a particular campus. Eighteen of these refer clearly to the regulation of student conduct (that is, to the custodial function of colleges), while only eleven are even remotely concerned with the fine arts. The Col-

116

lege Characteristics Index Form 457, which consists of 300 statements, includes only ten pertaining to the fine arts. Since the total of this inventory is intended to allow an assessment of the campus press, it may be instructive to consider those ten items that do pertain to the fine arts and to ponder what they imply:

A student who insists on analyzing and classifying art and music is likely to be regarded as a little odd.

When students get together they seldom talk about trends in art, music, or the theater.

More students here are in the humanities or social sciences than in the natural sciences.

There are paintings and statues of nudes on the campus.

Humanities and fine arts courses are often elected by students majoring in other areas.

Modern art and music get little attention here.

There is a lot of interest here in poetry, music, painting, sculpture, architecture, etc.

The library has paintings and phonograph records which circulate widely among the students.

Campus buildings, interiors, and landscaping are primarily formal and traditional rather than reflecting innovations and novelty.

Many famous people are brought to the campus for lectures, concerts, student discussions, etc.

Of course the fine arts are not always minimized in testing programs. The Educational Testing Service planned a series of college-level tests to enable colleges to assess student growth, effectiveness of programs, and credit earned elsewhere, and educational experiences gained in a noneducational setting. During the original planning in 1962 it was envisioned that the battery would consist of common, supplemental, and course examinations. For each type some provision was made for testing in the fine arts, as is indicated in Table 4. However, the emphasis, especially as envisioned in the common examination in the humanities, was historical rather than creative or aesthetic. In a sense the test was to reflect accurately the same pattern Fisher [18] found in courses in the humanities.

TABLE 4
COMPREHENSIVE COLLEGE TESTS

Common Examinations	Supplemental Examinations	Course Examinations
English Composition		American Literature
		English Literature
		20th Century European Literature
		Art
		Music
	Literature	French
Humanities		German
	Fine Arts	Russian
		Spanish
		Latin
		Western Civilization
		American History
	History	Modern European History
Social Sciences		Government
	Behavioral Sciences	Economics
		Sociology
		Psychology
		Anthropology
		Physics
		Chemistry
		Astronomy
	Physical Sciences	Geology
Natural Sciences		Botany
	Biological Sciences	Zoology
		Calculus
Mathematics		Finite Mathematics
		Statistics

Specifications for the Test in Humanities

Number of items: 100
Time required: 75 minutes
Special timing: none
Score report: total score

General Testing Objectives:
The scope of the humanities is here defined by the fields encompassed—literature, philosophy, and the arts—rather than by a more widespread or abstract conception. It may be useful to add, however, that it is believed that the humanities are properly the study of the forms in which man has left his record and that the study of these forms may enable men to reflect on possibilities in the human spirit that have at one time and another been urgent in men's minds. It is in the spirit of challenging the engagement of the student with these concerns that the Humanities Test is devised.

Test Content:
The wide-ranging nature of the humanities demands a test that will match the breadth of interest and knowledge of the student who is broadly educated in the intellectual and cultural worlds of mankind. The examination will require understanding beyond recall of isolated facts; it will deal not only with the student's range of reference (as described in the subsequent paragraph), but also with his knowledge of major figures, major movements, and major accomplishments, as well as with his ability to analyze, appraise, interpret, and describe, critically and afresh, the basic works of man that comprise the humanities. In addition, the test will measure his ability to understand and use fundamental terms and concepts to recognize formal elements and their relationships; to perceive organizing principles and their applications in particular works of art; to recognize distinguishing characteristics of historical periods, of particular schools and movements, of individual artists;

119

to understand the bases on which criticism can be applied.

Following are the approximate percentages to be devoted to certain major areas and topics.

1. *Content by Subject*	*Per Cent*
Painting and Drawing	10–15
Sculpture	8–10
Drama	5–7
Poetry	10–15
Fiction	5–8
Nonfiction	2–4
Music	8–12
Philosophy	13–18
Architecture	7–11
Cross-Field	15–20
2. *Content by Movement and Period*	*Per Cent*
Classical	10–15
Medieval	3–5
Renaissance	15–20
17th–18th Century	10–15
19th Century	15–20
20th Century	20–30
Other (Oriental, etc.)	5–10

Still another indication of the actual state of the fine and the performing arts in undergraduate education is revealed indirectly by a portion of the College Student Questionnaire.[19] This is intended to obtain standard biographical information and some evidence concerning attitudes and values from students before they enter college. A portion of the inventory presents four presumably prevailing philosophical points of view commonly found in American college students. In only one of the four does concern for the fine arts appear, and it does so in a context that suggests that anyone involved in such matters is likely to be a loner, a nonconformist, and very likely something of a bohemian.

120

On every college or university campus students hold a variety of attitudes about their own purposes and goals while at college. Such an attitude might be thought of as a personal philosophy of higher education. The following paragraphs are descriptive statements of four such "personal philosophies" which there is reason to believe are quite prevalent on American college campuses. As you read the four statements, attempt to determine how close each comes to *your own* philosophy of higher education.

Philosophy A: This philosophy emphasizes education essentially as preparation for an occupational future. Social or purely intellectual phases of campus life are relatively less important, although certainly not ignored. Concern with extracurricular activities and college traditions is relative small. Persons holding this philosophy are usually quite committed to particular fields of study and are in college primarily to obtain training for careers in their chosen fields.

Philosophy B: This philosophy, while it does not ignore career preparation, assigns greatest importance to scholarly pursuit of knowledge and understanding wherever the pursuit may lead. This philosophy entails serious involvement in course work or independent study *beyond* the minimum required. Social life and organized extracurricular activities are relatively unimportant. Thus, while other aspects of college life are not to be forsaken, this philosophy attaches greatest importance to interest in ideas, pursuit of knowledge, and cultivation of the intellect.

Philosophy C: This philosophy holds that besides occupational training and/or scholarly endeavor an important part of college life exists outside the classroom, laboratory, and library. Extracurricular activities, living-group functions, athletics, social life, rewarding friendships, and

121

loyalty to college traditions are important elements in one's college experience and necessary to the cultivation of the well-rounded person. Thus, while not excluding academic activities, this philosophy emphasizes the importance of the extracurricular side of college life.

Philosophy D: This is a philosophy held by the student who either consciously rejects commonly held value orientations in favor of his own, or who has not really decided what is to be valued and is in a sense searching for meaning in life. There is often deep involvement with ideas and art forms both in the classroom and in sources (often highly original and individualistic) in the wider society. There is little interest in business or professional careers; in fact, there may be a definite rejection of this kind of aspiration. Many facets of the college—organized extracurricular activities, athletics, traditions, the college administration—are ignored or viewed with disdain. In short, this philosophy may emphasize individualistic interests and styles, concern for personal identity, and often contempt for many aspects of organized society.

Although results are far from conclusive and are at present surrounded by no consistent theory, the fine arts do seem to attract a somewhat different sort of student than do the sciences or social sciences. Groups of students "reporting the most fears, worries, conflicts, and the like are almost always in the literary or fine arts fields . . . and the applied majors such as engineering, business, agriculture, education regularly show the fewest of these psychological problems." [20]

Although some institutions seem influential in encouraging the arts—the University of California, Los Angeles, is deemed the most potent influence in a resurgence of the arts in the Los Angeles area—and although some

122

educators truly want the collegiate scene to offer vibrant experiences in the arts—Harold Taylor, for example, remarks, "It is now clear that there is no other place than the schools and colleges for the arts to find a home; there is no more natural a place for the arts to be at home"— the impression one gets is that the undergraduate college shows little basic curricular concern for the arts.[21] Alvin Toffler claims that, "Almost unnoticed, the arts have moved in on higher education. A penetration has begun that is so enthusiastic and so widespread as to represent a basic change in the ecology of culture in America."[22] He supports his opinion by citing the growing number of arts festivals, artists, and writers-in-residence, lecture concert series, and training programs for professionals. However, the evidence thus far reviewed, which represents the phenomena to which most undergraduate students respond, suggests that the arts are still not regarded as central to the main purpose of the undergraduate college. If curricular patterns, testing programs designed to assess curricular outcomes, and opinions of professors are any indication, students are likely to regard the arts as something extra, something one does when there is nothing of importance to do. A summary of attitudes of professional faculty members toward the liberal arts reflects this.

> In addition to the strong preference for those courses having direct relevance for particular technical fields, there was a preference shared by faculty from all fields for those subjects developing particular intellectual skills. Thus, mathematics, English composition, and speech were seen as desirable requirements by substantial majorities of all professional faculty members, regardless of their specialties. This was in contrast to the relatively small number of people who would see art, music, philosophy and religion as desirable re-

quirements for students in technical and professional fields.[23]

While at this moment we do not know whether students with interests or talents in the fine or performing arts have actually been penalized, they have certainly not been encouraged. First of all, the relationship between artistic or musical talent and academic aptitude is low to negative. When this is coupled with the fact that the two most frequently used selective devices for college admission are high school rank in class and scores on an academic aptitude test, the basis for inference is well established. Then, when one examines the condition of the fine and performing arts in America's secondary schools, one finds very little reason to believe that students are encouraged to think as seriously about the arts as about mathematics, science, or even foreign language. The evidence for such a statement is quite pervasive.

A survey of the current curriculum reform movement reveals at least three different weaknesses. First, program development in social sciences, humanities (especially the arts, health and physical education) is as yet only embryonic at both elementary and secondary levels of education. There is some activity in all of these fields but it does not compare in intensity or accomplishment with what has already transpired in mathematics, physics, chemistry and biology. Should this situation continue, it will result in an imbalance of the curriculum and disproportional allocation of human and material resources.[24]

Generally the curricula of most high schools assign only a minor place to the fine arts. In English and language courses students will have some contact with poetry and drama. They may take a course in music appreciation in junior high school. But in senior high school courses in the arts have become elective and will be taken only by students with pronounced talent or, one must suspect, by those judged incapable of pursuing an academic program. When participation is encouraged, it is done so in such an extracurricular context as a band or an orchestra; only on occasion is the respectability of academic credit given such efforts. The dominant intellectual activity is usually the mere memorization of specific facts about artists, works of art, and technique. Where artistic expression is tolerated, as in some courses in painting, it becomes an emotional self-indulgence rather than a disciplined use of a medium to reach for and express some form of human truth.[25]

There are, of course, differences between art and music offered in secondary schools. Nearly all (95 per cent) secondary schools offer music, and the teachers are generally well trained. However, well over half of all high school graduates have taken less than a full year of music. Students not majoring in music are allowed one or two credits out of the sixteen required to graduate, but must often choose from among several music alternatives. School bands and choruses are the most popular courses. Art is less fortunate. It clearly does not hold a major place in the secondary curriculum. Only 14.9 per cent of high school students elect to take any art, while two-thirds of smaller high schools do not even offer art. Generally art, when offered, is called general art so that students simply sample various media. Although there is some slight increase in art enrollments, art as offered at present does not compare with music in the interest it holds for secondary students.[26]

The dilettante quality of work in the arts is reflected by a description of a progressive school in California.

> Kennedy and his staff have instituted some para-academic enterprises to overcome the students' rootlessness and anonymity and to generate excitement about the bigger world, a world sometimes hard to reach and perceive in the confusion of southern California. In addition to Great Books there is a venture called Seminar in which the monthly discussion sessions are supplemented by monthly trips to cultural events in Los Angeles including, even in this land of Birchers, a rehearsal of the Leningrad Ballet. Dramatic groups perform regularly at Lowell, and every spring the school runs an ambitious festival of fine arts which includes dance, drama, music and art. But the shaping motif of these activities is not so much the development of rigorous descriptive in the arts and literature as it is exposure to the Good Life, like instruction in swimming or tennis.[27]

Although across the country secondary schools have been taken out of their former lethargy by the launching of Sputnik, pressure for college admission, the civil rights movement, and the knowledge explosion, the effects have been felt chiefly in fields other than the arts. The new sciences, mathematics, the oral-aural approach to language, the wider use of paperback books, uses of induction in teaching, and education for the culturally deprived, the advanced student, and the mentally retarded—these are the areas in which innovation is rampant.[28]

Reasons for this are not hard to discover. Almost half of the nation's elementary teachers, in schools where art is taught, need not have had course work in art. Many secondary school art teachers have had little or no formal training in art. Even in areas that can and do afford well-

126

trained and talented teachers, art and music are not legally required courses, hence are among the first to be eliminated when economics are considered. Even in common schools, enjoined to teach drawing, the amount of time to be so devoted is not specified, hence rests with the discretion of the Board of Trustees.

Further, in states such as California, where the teaching of foreign language is mandatory, the resulting crowding of the curriculum virtually ensures that the fine arts will be minimized. And in academic high schools with a large number of college-bound students, even a three-year elective sequence in art or music becomes "a refuge for those students who cannot conform to do the academic requirements for college entrance and/or business education." Students electing a one-year course seem typically to be in search of a "snap" elective to meet minimum graduation requirements. "Art does not have status in the hierarchy of school subjects and is often not considered for evaluation in competition for academic honors." Rarely are art or music courses required for graduation, and well under a half of all high school students enroll for nonrequired art courses.[29]

Nor are the reasons for the low estate of the arts in secondary schools any more difficult to discover. The educational establishment reflects latent tendencies and desires in the society, and the Jacksonian distrust of art and aesthetes runs deep. There will from time to time be pleas that the arts play an important role in school. "To develop interest in music through experiences commonly had with radio and juke boxes is to miss the opportunity to develop interest in music of greater variety and higher quality. The school cannot forego the latter, anymore than it can afford not to develop appreciation and understanding of aesthetic principles in art and literature. Again this is a

127

problem centered on the development of instruction as it should be related to widely varying student interests and abilities."[30] Generally, however, the schools listen to other drummers.

The task force of the National Commission on Teacher Education and Professional Standards sought to advance professorial standards for the profession.[30] Their report asks that educators be liberally educated, aware of advanced and technical knowledge, independent enough to make far-reaching decisions, and committed to moral and intellectual excellence. It further argues strongly for general education for all teachers that will be relevant to the teacher's role as individual, citizen, and professional educator. This general education should develop understanding of the various divisions of knowledge, the skills of logical and clear thinking, and communication skills; an awareness of his own value system; and a perspective from which to regard his own specialization. The important point is that never once are the concepts of beauty or aesthetics even mentioned. The document could well serve as justification for a teacher preparation program consisting of history, science, language, and social science plus professional and specialized courses.

To the pronouncement of a major educational commission is added the dry self-assurance of education's elder statesman, James B. Conant.[32] Conant equates foreign languages, art, music, and physical education as posing quite specific and common problems. The music or art teacher must be a specialist brought in to take over an elementary classroom for an hour or more each week, or to offer an *elective* course in high school. Such teachers face an undefined task, partly because of their fields and partly because the American public is not sure why such instruction should even be given in public schools. This uncertainty is reflected in the amount of time assigned to the subjects and the varying practices as to the optional nature of the work. The emphasis on science and mathematics since Sputnik is generally believed to have reduced the amount of time the average or better-than-average student spends on art and music. So pronounced has this become that art and music teachers have developed inferiority complexes about their position in competing for students' time and seem to be trying to upgrade their specialties. Generally, Conant believes that artistic or musical talent can be detected quite early and that only those students who have it should be encouraged to specialize. As far as advanced training for public school teachers in the arts is concerned, he doubts "if the instruction in this field at the graduate level is sufficiently developed to warrant further time to the improvement of skills. The equivalent of a major in art history together with psychology might be considered." [33] Conant makes his point even more strenuously in an earlier work.[34] He would have all applicants for graduate and professional school pass rigorous examinations in academic subjects somewhat comparable to those required for entry into European universities. Those who enter the professional schools must be among the academically talented, who would be identified by academic aptitude tests and, of course, earlier academic preformance. In high school these students would have taken four years of English, three each of history and mathematics. For electives they should have taken more mathematics, science, and social science, and a four-year sequence in foreign language. For the less talented other programs would be offered (presumably art and music among them) that should allow such lesser mortals to have some personal satisfaction and to do useful work.

Even when one leaves educators and educational

129

theorists and seeks to determine the values of high school students, the climate for the fine and performing arts is no more comfortable. The peer culture of high school and college students is gradually being recognized as the most potent educational force. A perceptive high school principal can, along with his teachers, incline peer group values slightly toward the educational values he wishes to develop. But a principal who is not perceptive leaves the molding of standards to the teenagers themselves, and their standards do not currently involve in any appreciable way a concern for the arts. While obviously the values or styles of different schools vary, there are also strong similarities. Every school has a leading crowd in which membership is determined by being an athlete, dancing well, owning a car, being a good date, and liking parties. Although the in-group in many schools will be college-bound youth, academic success is not explicitly related to whether or not students are popular. In an entire analysis of adolescents and the schools, no concern for any except the most popular of the arts is ever mentioned.

Coleman's generalization [35] is given additional support from questionnaire data obtained from high school seniors planning to enter one of twenty-three different institutions in the fall of 1963.[36] Of these students, 82 per cent indicated no or slight interest in modern art, and 85 per cent claimed to know nothing or very little about the history of architecture. Also, 85 per cent were familiar with either none or one of the works of Pergolesi, Mahler, or Stravinsky. A similar percentage knew nothing or only a small amount about the history of painting. However, almost half of this group did claim to have had a deep personal reaction to a work of art during the past year, and slightly over half derived quite a bit or a great deal of pleasure from classical music.

What has been described thus far is a situation in which the fine and performing arts are given little curricular expression in colleges and universities. Further, these matters do not appear central in secondary schools or in the thinking of college-bound adolescents. It would be unreasonable, in light of these factors, to assume that interest or talent in the arts would help students be admitted to college, or that the arts figure in any appreciable way in the college admissions process. Indeed, an opposite influence seems more than plausible: that is, an expressed and active interest in the arts would generally hurt a student's chances for admission to an academically oriented college.

First, if prospective students were to judge their chances of gaining admission to a selective college on the frequently published criteria, they would not value interest or talent in the fine or performing arts very highly. Typical criteria are: "Applicants' scholastic ability and preparation, character, and health"; "College preparatory subjects are preferable"; "At least twelve units in the following subjects: English, foreign language, history, mathematics, and laboratory science"; "Selected on the basis of their secondary school record and grade average, their performance on the SAT, and such additional factors as the recommendation of the secondary school counselor or principal, and a personal interview"; "Twelve must be in strictly academic courses." [37]

If students were to judge from the form and substance of commonly used admission tests, they would similarly be disillusioned about the importance of the fine and performing arts. The College Entrance Examination Board Program, for example, lists the Scholastic Aptitude Test designed to measure the verbal and mathematical skills necessary for success in college and achievement tests in history and the social studies, biology, chemistry, Eng-

131

lish composition, European history and world culture, French, German, Hebrew, Latin, mathematics, physics, Russian, and Spanish. Applicants are expected to take three from this list. Obviously there are no tests available in the arts, nor does the substance of examinations that could remotely impinge on the arts reflect concern for these areas. The Achievement Examination in English composition, for example, presents students with 100 different sentences or paragraphs, only three of which refer at all to the fine arts, and one of those suggests that the fine arts were refused a position of equality with other subjects within the university. The European history and world culture test consists of 100 questions, only one of which concerns the arts. That question asks students to indicate the period in which a picture was painted. And the American history and social studies test has no question that would suggest that the arts had in any way been involved in American civilization.

Increasingly, the typical admissions process is for students to apply to one or more colleges and submit aptitude test scores from one of the major national testings programs such as the American College Testing Program or the Admissions Program of the College Entrance Examination Board. The college, on receipt of high school records, test scores, and recommendations, then makes decisions, at least three-quarters of which are so clear-cut that a secretary could make them. Students in this group are clearly the sort that the college either does or does not want. But discretion is needed to decide among the remaining quarter. A review of how admissions officers in 376 colleges handled borderline cases [38] makes it quite clear that the fine and performing arts are not really of much significance in the secondary school, the college and

132

university, or in the processes by which students move from one educational level to another. Schools and colleges have been and are preoccupied with developing one sort of ability that may or may not be relevant to work in or enjoyment of the arts. Assuming that this condition should be changed, what should a federal agency do to bring about desired changes?

First, it should be recognized that tests themselves are not at fault. They generally reflect informed opinion on the present state of the curriculum. While within limits changing the substance of tests can force faculties to change what they teach, the available domain in which this can happen is relatively small. Thus, an area test on the Graduate Record Examination in the humanities can encourage colleges to enrich their offerings in Western civilization. However, if a major testing program devised tests covering the plastic arts and ballet without considering actual practice, the tests would remain unused. The Cooperative Study of General Education, the Progressive Education Association Eight Year Study, and the Cooperative Study of Evaluation in General Education all created new tests for worthwhile outcomes of collegiate education. Unfortunately, the profession as a whole was not ready for such materials, and the tests exist now only in a few archives.

Nor will simply exhorting college professors and secondary school boards and principals persuade them that the arts should be featured more prominently. The Max Raffertys and the discipline-oriented faculty members can destroy such pleas either on the ground of financial expediency (why waste dollars on frills?) or on the ground that time spent in the arts denies students the rigorous training that will make them better scientists, doctors, or

133

whatever. Until the virtues of the arts can be demonstrated as dramatically as Sputnik demonstrated the powers of science, progress is likely to be slow.

However, a few steps can be taken. First, a number of colleges, mostly of the experimental variety, have made the arts an essential element of campus life. Colleges such as Goddard, Bennington, Sarah Lawrence, and Stephens could be studied to determine how the arts have moved to such significance.

Second, organizations such as the American Association for Higher Education, the Association for General and Liberal Studies, and the American Council on Education might use one of their annual conferences to debate the issues involved in finding an appropriate role for the arts. In this connection, the Educational Policies Commission might be invited to make a formal statement on the role of the arts in the life of contemporary man.

Third, the experimental possibilities suggested by some of the unknowns revealed in this paper might be studied in collaboration with such agencies as the College Entrance Examination Board. The CEEB is constantly seeking to explore barriers to access to higher education, and would beyond doubt be concerned if some of its own programs discouraged students of specific talents from entering college. Further, because of the prestige of its admissions and advanced placement tests, a change in form of those examinations could actually force a change in curricular practice. Even a replication of the Eight Year Study might be attempted to determine what actually would happen to artistically inclined students if they matriculated into an academically oriented institution.

Then, too, massive national curriculum studies in the arts, as large as the School Mathematics Study Group

or the Physical Science Study Program, could be under-
taken. If the best professional teachers and students in the
arts could work at developing new materials, schools
would be better supplied with materials, and leaders
would emerge who within a decade could begin to affect
educational practice.

In one sense these suggestions are only palliatives.
What is really needed is a massive demonstration that the
fine and performing arts are truly central in the lives of
people, or could be if allowed to so become. If the arts are
this important, this fact could be shown in several ways.

1. If students who are deeply exposed to artistic
experiences in the early years of college do as well
in subsequent education and work as those not so
exposed, enjoy life greatly, and lead longer lives
of greater freedom from personality disorders, some
inferences would be possible.

2. If long exposure to the arts results in greater
creativity in an individual's vocation or avocation,
other important inferences could be drawn.

3. If long exposure to various arts results in greater
altruistic contribution to the life of society, still
other inferences are possible.

These are all experimental approaches. Other approaches are possible. First, the lives of students who have
attended such colleges as Bennington, Sarah Lawrence, or
Stephens could be examined in depth to see what effects
exposure to the arts has seemingly had. Newcomb has done
this for Bennington students, and it is clear that the arts
do make a difference.[39] Then the role the arts have played
in the lives of creative people could be examined and
widely discussed; Torrence, Getzels, and McKinnon would
each have relevant data. Then, too, the case records and

135

insights of psychiatrists could be examined to determine how the arts have helped or hindered gaining personal insight.

These approaches still are not as arresting as the launching of Sputnik, which demanded that science become the central fact of contemporary life. Probably no such demonstration could be planned or engineered, but some approaches are suggested through analogy. The economic base of life was clearly and powerfully demonstrated by a small man working alone in the British Museum. The concept of evolution was made explicit when an ineffective person was given a chance to take a sea voyage. A proud, lonely doctor in Vienna came up with a description of the irrational forces that shape so much of human life. Another man who was not very good at experiments calculated a base that led to unlocking atomic power. Now, is it possible to identify some people who have relevant training and experience and provide them with the time to explore in detail the whole matter of the arts in human experience? Clearly there are expressed insights. What is required is that someone master them in the hope that a formulation of major importance might emerge.

References

1. "The Performing Arts: Problems and Prospects," *Arts in Society*, 1965, *3*:343–344.
2. Dwight MacDonald, *Against the American Grain* (New York: Random House, 1962).
3. James A. Perkins, *The University in Transition* (Princeton, N.J.: Princton University Press, 1966).
4. Alvin Toffler, *The Culture Consumers* (Baltimore, Penguin Books, 1965).

5. Harold Taylor, "Symposium Statement," *Arts in Society*, 3, Number 4 (Madison, Wisc.: University of Wisconsin, Summer 1966); and *Music and Art in the Public Schools*, Research Monograph 1963-M3 (Washington, D.C.: National Education Association, 1963).

6. Bernard Berelson and Gary Steiner, *Human Behavior: An Inventory of Scientific Findings* (New York: Harcourt, 1964), pp. 228–229.

7. Kenneth R. Beittel, "Art," in C. W. Harris (Ed.), *Encyclopedia of Educational Research* (New York: Macmillan, 1960), p. 83.

8. Joseph W. Cohen (Ed.), *The Superior Student in American Higher Education* (New York: McGraw-Hill, 1966).

9. *Ibid.*

10. Daniel Bell, *The Reforming of General Education* (New York: Columbia University Press, 1966).

11. James A. Fisher, *The Humanities in General Education* (Dubuque, Iowa: William C. Brown, 1960).

12. *Ibid.*, pp. 10–12.

13. Bell, *op. cit.*, pp. 291–292.

14. A. Edwin Anderson, *The Humanities in the Colleges and Universities of the South* (Atlanta: Southern Regional Education Board, 1961).

15. *Ibid.*, pp. 17–18.

16. Harold A. Haswell and Clarence B. Lindquist, *Undergraduate Curriculum Patterns* (Washington, D.C.: U.S. Office of Education, 1966).

17. *Testing Programs—Service Program* (Princeton, N.J.: Educational Testing Service, 1963).

18. Fisher, *op. cit.*

19. Educational Testing Service, Princton, N.J.

20. Carl Bereiter and Mervin B. Freedman, "Fields of Study and the People in Them," in N. Sanford (Ed.), *The American College* (New York: Wiley, 1962).

21. Taylor, *op. cit.*

22. Toffler, *op. cit.*

23. Paul L. Dressel, Lewis B. Mayhew, and Earl J. McGrath, *The Liberal Arts as Viewed by Faculty Members in Professional Schools* (New York: Teachers College, Columbia University, 1959).

24. John I. Goodlad, *School Curriculum Reform in the United States* (New York: Fund for the Advancement of Education, 1964).
25. Maurity Johnson, Jr., *American Secondary Schools* (New York: Harcourt, 1965).
26. *Music and Art in the Public Schools, op. cit.*
27. Peter Schrag, *Voices in the Classroom* (Boston: Beacon Press, 1965).
28. *Ibid.,* p. 3.
29. Ida Shimans, "The Cultural Explosion: Challenge to Art Education," *Art Education,* June 1966, pp. 3–8.
30. Elmer R. Smith, *Teacher Education: A Reappraisal* (New York: Harper, 1962).
31. Margaret Lindsey (Ed.), *New Horizons for the Teaching Profession* (Washington, D.C.: National Education Association, 1961).
32. James B. Conant, *The Education of American Teachers* (New York: McGraw-Hill, 1963).
33. *Ibid.*
34. James B. Conant, *Slums and Suburbs* (New York: McGraw-Hill, 1961).
35. James S. Coleman, *Adolescents and the Schools* (New York: Basic Books, 1965).
36. *A Summary of Responses to College Student Questionnaires: Part I, Experimented Form 284C* (Princeton, N.J.: Educational Testing Service, 1964).
37. *The College Handbook* (New York: College Entrance Examination Board, 1966–67).
38. George Nash, "Admissions Criteria as Reported by Admissions Offices" (New York: Columbia University, 1965). Unpublished.
39. Theodore M. Newcomb, *Personality and Social Change* (New York: Dryden Press, 1943).

VII

Lawrence E. Dennis

Recommendations
for Action

The arts can win priority on the agenda of American higher education in the 1970's only by concerted action on the part of professional organizations, federal and state governments, national foundations, educational research and service associations, and educational institutions themselves—the schools, junior colleges, colleges, and universities where young people and adults seek artistic outlets for creativity. No one of these institutions or agencies can do the job alone: lowering the barriers and increasing access to the arts on our campuses can only be a collective responsibility.

Of course innovations and experiments can and must—as always—guide the way. But it would be naïve to assume that innovations and experiments—such as an exciting approach to the teaching of the arts at the second-

139

ary level (for example, Phillips Academy at Andover), or the development of an internationally famous instructional program in the arts in a multiversity (for example, music at Indiana University), or the building of an imaginative arts curriculum for adults in the area of continuing education (for example, University College at Syracuse University)—could alone measurably affect the status of the arts in education nationally. What is needed is a long-range, intensive, coordinated effort to win for the arts a central position in the educational experience. Such an effort could be planned and developed by a large number of agencies and institutions with a better-than-even chance of success.

Specifically, what is required is an action program designed to achieve a maximum national impact within a period of half a decade or so—a program not unlike those which in recent years have revolutionized the teaching of science at the secondary level, have secured the passage by Congress of the Public Broadcasting Act, and have brought into being, with federal and foundation support, institutes or centers of urban studies on major campuses in every section of the country. Programs of this kind, to be viable, require ideas, commitment, leadership, objectives, planning, funds, and a framework for organization. The effectiveness of such programs, from a national viewpoint, stems in no small way from the willingness of educators and laymen from various parts of the country to put aside their special institutional concerns and work cooperatively toward an overriding goal.

The recommendations that follow, taken together, could constitute the preliminary outline for such a program for the arts in education. These proposals represent those steps that—in the judgment of the AAHE Arts Study Project staff and the AAHE Executive Committee—could

140

fashion a new and much more receptive climate for the arts both inside and outside higher education. They are put forth with the idea that concerted action is needed now, throughout the educational community, if the arts are to develop the capacity for growth and self-renewal so essential for survival in the modern academic world.

Recommendation One: Establishment of a National Commission on the Arts in Education

There should be established within the immediate future, with financial support from educational foundations and the National Endowment on the Arts, a National Commission on the Arts in Education. Such a commission should be sponsored jointly by the American Association for Higher Education, the American Council on Education's Commission on Academic Affairs, the Association of American Colleges, and the National Council of the Arts in Education. The commission should function for an extended period—two to three years—and should be perceived as the instrument whereby public and professional attention can be drawn to the problem of access and barriers to the arts. The commission should be broadly representative of the entire field of education, the fine and performing arts, and the general public. It should have a high-level administrative and research staff, and it should hold hearings in various regions of the United States to assay the major issues and questions facing education in the arts. Through the sponsorship of hearings, conferences, and seminars, and through the issuance of periodic reports of research studies, the commission could evolve guidelines useful to schools and institutions of higher learning, to governmental agencies, to professional organizations, and to educational foundations.

Prototypes for the establishment of such a commission exist—in the Carnegie Commission on Public Broad-

devote a portion of their annual budgets to help establish the centers.

Recommendation Four: Development of new courses, curricula, and instructional materials in the arts, at both the secondary school and college levels

Throughout secondary and higher education, physics and biology courses have been completely reformed and revamped in recent years, thanks to the organized efforts of leaders in those disciplines who recognized the inadequacies of old instructional materials and old teaching methods. The same kind of reorganizing could and should be done for the arts.

Professional organizations, again, should band together to make it possible for a first-class team of teachers and scholars to devote whatever time is required for the analysis of current procedures and materials and for producing recommendations on the changes that will be needed to present courses in the arts more effectively to more people. Such analyses and recommendations should be devoted to arts courses designed for the general student as well as for those students who intend to enter the arts professionally. The National Endowment for the Arts and the major educational foundations should underwrite such a curriculum reform study, and it should be accorded top priority by leaders in the arts professions.

Recommendation Five: Research on public attitudes toward the arts

At a time when the nation is engaged in a reordering of its social, economic, and political priorities, too little is known about the way people feel about the fine arts. How widely understood is the role that schools and colleges should play in building a reservoir of artistic talent and in furthering artistic appreciation? Is support for state and federal government activity in the arts narrowly based or widespread? Would the public generally accord the arts a higher or lower priority in a scale of national values than, say, the space program or highway development or supersonic air travel?

The Educational Policies Commission of the National Education Association incorporated a proposal for more research relating to attitudes toward the arts in its statement, "The Role of the Fine Arts in Education," issued in 1968. Such research, said the Educational Policies Commission, should

> consider more than the usual head-counting of concert attendance and participation in educational programs in the arts. Its main purpose would be to answer such questions as these: To what extent is the current American "craze" for the arts a status-oriented phenomenon? To what degree is education in the arts regarded by educators as a process of conveying content or skills? What justifications do students give for the time they spend in various kinds of programs in the arts? What are students' attitudes toward subjectivity and the future of usefulness and work?

Only by uniting now to support a research effort of the kind suggested can universities, foundations, and government agencies formulate realistic goals for education in the fine arts a decade hence.

Appendix

Authors and Participants in AAHE Arts Project Seminars

Clinton Adams, College of Fine Arts, University of New Mexico

John H. Allen, Dean, University of Southern Mississippi

Scarvie Anderson, Educational Testing Service, Princeton, New Jersey

Helen Bidwell, Assistant to the Director of Educational Programs, National Endowment for the Arts, Washington, D.C.

Kathryn Bloom, Director, Arts and Humanities Program, U.S. Office of Education

Robert S. Bolles, Dean, College of Architecture and Fine Arts, University of Florida

Erling Brauner, Chairman, Department of Art, Michigan State University

Robert L. Briggs, Dean, College of Fine Arts and Professional Studies, University of Tulsa

William Brinkley, Director of Admissions, The Johns Hopkins University

146

Henry A. Bruinsma, Dean, College of Fine Arts, Arizona State University

Mayo Bryce, President, Moore College of Art

Leonard F. Cain, Dean, College of Arts and Sciences, The Catholic University of America

Allen C. Cannon, Director, School of Music, Bradley University

James M. Carpenter, Professor of Fine Arts, Colby College

Richard Cervene, Chairman, Department of Art, Grinnell College

Norman Charles, Dean of Humanities, Millersville State College

Albert Christ-Janer, Dean, School of Art and Design, Pratt Institute

F. Donald Clark, Dean, College of Fine Arts, University of Oklahoma

Barbara Clough, Director of Admissions, Wellesley College

Frank B. Cookson, Dean, School of Fine Arts, University of Connecticut

Ted S. Cooper, Executive Director, Association of College Admissions Counselors, Evanston, Illinois

Jed H. Davis, University Theater, The University of Kansas

Royden B. Davis, S.J., Dean, College of Arts and Sciences, Georgetown University

Lawrence E. Dennis, Chancellor, Rhode Island State System of Higher Education, and Director, AAHE Arts Study Project

Charles M. Dorn, Executive Secretary, National Art Education Association, Washington, D.C.

E. W. Doty, Dean, College of Fine Arts, University of Texas

147

Charles A. Dunn, Jr., Director of Admissions, Rhode Island School of Design

Henry S. Dyer, Vice President, Educational Testing Service, Princeton, N.J.

Earl E. Edgar, Dean, Graduate School, Youngstown State University

Edmund B. Feldman, Professor of Art, University of Georgia

Charles L. Gary, Executive Secretary (Elect), Music Educators National Conference, Washington, D.C.

Roger Gilmore, Acting Dean, School of Art Institute of Chicago

Thomas B. A. Godfrey, Dean, Graduate School of Fine Arts, University of Pennsylvania

Sister Mary Grell, President, College of St. Benedict

Harlan P. Hanson, Director, Advanced Placement Program, College Entrance Examination Board, New York, New York

Robert Hargreaves, Head, Department of Music, Ball State University

Jack Harrison, Christian Faith and Higher Education Institute, East Lansing, Michigan

Bartlett H. Hayes, Jr., Director, Addison Gallery of American Art, Phillips Academy

Jules Heller, Dean, College of Arts and Architecture, The Pennsylvania State University

Sally Hellyer, Chairman, College Committee, San Francisco Art Institute

James K. Hitt, Registrar, The University of Kansas

Francis Hodge, Department of Drama, The University of Texas

Harlan Hoffa, Division of Laboratories and Research Development, U.S. Office of Education

George Howerton, Dean, School of Music, Northwestern University

Kenneth E. Hudson, Dean, School of Fine Arts, Washington University

Robert L. Hull, College of Fine Arts, University of Arizona

C. B. Hunt, Jr., Dean of the Graduate School, George Peabody College for Teachers

Abbott Kaplan, President, State University of New York, College at Purchase

James Paul Kennedy, Director, School of Music, Bowling Green State University

Walter D. Knight, University of California, Berkeley

Vanett Lawler, Executive Secretary, Music Educators National Conference, Washington, D.C.

Warner Lawson, Dean, College of Fine Arts, Howard University

David A. Ledet, Executive Secretary, National Association of Schools of Music, National Association of Schools of Art, Washington, D.C.

Harold Luce, Acting Director, School of Music, Ohio State University

Dorothy G. Madden, University of Maryland

Stanley Madeja, Art Education Specialist, Arts and Humanities Program, U.S. Office of Education

David Mallery, Director of Studies, National Association of Independent Schools, Philadelphia, Pennsylvania

Raymond Mannoni, Dean, School of Fine Arts, University of Southern Mississippi

Fred Martin, Director of the College, San Francisco Art Institute

Jacquelyn A. Mattfeld, Dean of the College, Sarah Lawrence College

149

Edward L. Mattil, Head, Department of Art Education, College of Education, The Pennsylvania State University

David Matz, Executive Assistant to the President, Hampshire College

Lewis B. Mayhew, Professor of Education, Stanford University

Bernard McGregor, Creative Arts Center, West Virginia University

Barbara Miller, Dean of Admissions, Maryland Institute College of Art

Eugene S. Mills, Dean, College of Liberal Arts, University of New Hampshire

Clark Mitze, Director of State and Community Operations, National Endowment for the Arts, Washington, D.C.

Jack S. Morrison, Dean, School of Fine Arts and Architecture, Ohio University

James Niblock, Chairman, Department of Music, Michigan State University

M. B. Ogle, Jr., Dean, School of Humanities, Social Sciences and Education, Purdue University

Leon Pacala, Dean, College of Arts and Sciences, Bucknell University

Garland G. Parker, Vice Provost for Admissions and Records, University of Cincinnati

Nelson M. Parkhurst, Registrar, Purdue University

Richard R. Perry, Director, Office of Admissions and Records, The University of Toledo

Donald E. Rhoades, Dean of Admissions and Records, University of Iowa

Norman L. Rice, Dean, College of Fine Arts, Carnegie Mellon University

William A. Richardson, Associate Dean, Oberlin Conservatory of Music

150

Lee Rigsby, Dean, College of the Arts, The Ohio State University

James E. Russell, Educational Policies Commission, National Education Association, Washington, D.C.

Jasper M. San Fratello, Chairman of Admissions, School of Art Institute of Chicago

Allen Sapp, Chairman, Music Department, State University of New York at Buffalo

G. Kerry Smith, Executive Secretary, American Association for Higher Education

Ralph A. Smith, Associate Professor of Aesthetic Education, College of Fine and Applied Arts, University of Illinois

James R. Spence, Director of Admissions Program, State University of New York at Albany

T. Sherman Stanford, Dean of Admissions, The Pennsylvania State University

Martin Stearns, Dean, College of Liberal Arts, Wayne State University

Edwin E. Stein, Dean, School of Fine and Applied Arts, Boston University

Leon Stein, Dean, School of Music, DePaul University

David C. Stewart, Director of Programs in Education and Public Media, National Endowment for the Arts, Washington, D.C.

Frank S. Stillings, School of Fine and Applied Arts, Central Michigan University

David L. Stone, Dean, College of Music, Temple University

Margery Thompson, Center for the Study of Instruction, National Education Association, Washington, D.C.

Paul A. Varg, Dean, College of Arts and Letters, Michigan State University

Himie Voxman, Director, School of Music, University of Iowa

Oliver W. Wagner, Director of Admissions and Registrar, Washington University

Edward S. Welch, Educational Policies Commission, National Education Association, Washington, D.C.

William West, Stephens College Playhouse

Stephen A. Whealton, Educational Policies Commission, National Education Association, Washington, D.C.

Lorin F. Wheelwright, Dean, College of Fine Arts and Communications, Brigham Young University

Ralph L. Wickiser, Director, Graduate Programs in Art and Design, Pratt Institute

Raphael Wilson, C.S.C., Director, Office of Admissions and Scholarships, University of Notre Dame

Cliff W. Wing, Office of the Provost, Duke University

William Whybrew, Dean, College of Fine and Applied Arts, Northern Illinois University

Frederick L. Wormald, Vice President, Association of American Colleges, Washington, D.C.

Index

A

Admissions practices, 3–4, 7–9, 65, 88–102, 109–111, 131–133; Carnegie Unit, 11–13; conditional admissions, 8–10
Admissions tests, 84, 85–88, 116–122, 131–133; effect of bias of judges on, 97–102
Advanced Placement Program, 116
Advanced Test in Fine Arts, 86–87
American Association for Higher Education, 2, 18, 134; AAHE Arts Study Project, 6–16
American College Testing Program, 87, 132
American Council on Education, 134
ANASTASI, A., 90, 93, 103
ANDERSON, A. E., 114, 137
Architectural Aptitude Test, 93
ARNSTINE, D., 39–40
Artist: reasons for creating, 33–35, 47–48; vs. scholar, 45–49; social concepts of, 56–58; as teachers, 72–73
Artists-in-residence, 62, 64–65, 72–73
Arts: college testing and, 82–103; as communication, 44–46;

Arts (*Cont.*):
and democratic values, 21–39; discrimination against, 14, 46–47, 122–124; as education, 44–58; as end in itself, 21, 29–30; functions, 38–39; and individualism, 21–22, 28–29; schism between (a) arts and philosophy, 47, (b) theory and practice, 43–44; status of research and experimentation in, 76–79; teaching of, 27–28, 60–80
Arts education programs: admission policies (*See* Admissions practices); art requirements, 113–115; artist vs. scholar, 45–49; attitudes toward arts programs of (a) educators, 128–129, (b) faculty, 115, (c) peers, 130, (d) public, 127–128, 144–145; as balance to science and technology, 68–69; creativity test centers, proposed, 143–144; cultural explosion and, 65–68; as enrichment, 16–17, 52–56, 135–136; government and private agencies in, 4–5; grading vs. testing, 95–102; guidance counselors in, 5, 16; incor-

153

155

157